Prima Materia
volume 3

Stories We Tell Ourselves

Writings from the Hudson Valley, New York

~

Edited by Brent Robison

Prima Materia
Volume 3

Copyright © 2004 by Bliss Plot Press

Each selection herein copyright © 2004 by the author

ALL RIGHTS RESERVED

No part of this book may be reproduced or transmitted in any form or by any means, electronic or mechanical, including photocopying, recording, or by any information storage or retrieval system, without prior written permission from the copyright owner unless such copying is expressly permitted by federal copyright law. The publisher is not authorized to grant permission for further uses of copyrighted selections printed in this book. Permission must be obtained from the individual copyright owners identified herein. Requests for permission should be addressed to the publisher.

Acknowledgment:
"Flukenschweilers: Lovely Fire" by Paloma J. R. Kopp appeared previously in a different form in *The Phoenicia Times*.

Published by Bliss Plot Press, PO Box 68, Mt. Tremper, NY 12457
Editor/Publisher: Brent Robison
Associate Publisher: Wendy Klein

Submissions: Unsolicited manuscripts should include a self-addressed, stamped envelope (SASE) or an e-mail address; otherwise we cannot respond. For submission guidelines, send an SASE with your request, or visit www.blissplotpress.com.

ISBN 0-9718908-4-6
ISSN 1538-9553

Printed in the United States of America

Cover design by Brent Robison
Photo: "Night Vision" © Wendy Klein, 1997

The Hudson River Valley

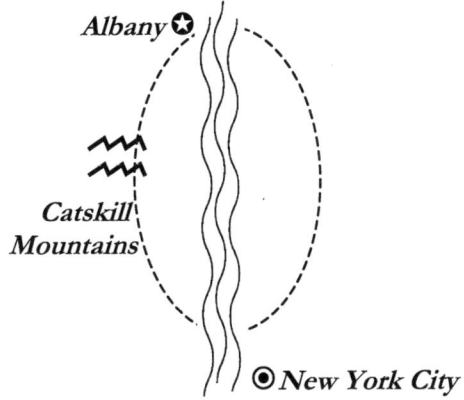

In 1609, Henry Hudson sailed the Half Moon up the river that would one day bear his name. He called it the River of Mountains and wrote of its valley, "It is as pleasant a land as one can tread upon." Washington Irving later made local folk tales famous with "The Legend of Sleepy Hollow" and "Rip Van Winkle," capturing a dark magic that most certainly hides in these hills. A surprising number of arts colonies and spiritual retreats have found refuge in these wooded valleys for over a century. Today, rumor has it that the region claims more "artists" per capita than any comparable area in the country. And UFOs as well.

With "The City," the center of the world, just an easy jaunt downriver, and world-class culture swarming north to our doorstep, we can still enjoy the sight of a black bear eating berries in the backyard. There's something in the air here, or the soil, or the water. There's an energy in the Hudson Valley that has called creative spirits from all over the world. There's serious talent here, working in secret in these woods and river towns. This book gives a sampling of the stories we have to tell.

To find the philosopher's stone:
"Pray, read, read, read, read again, labor, and discover."
—*Mutus Liber*
(Wordless Book)
1677

Prima Materia
volume 3

⸻ Contents ⸻

Introduction	9
Endings and Beginnings	
Life Full of Light: The Confessions of Arthur Rimbaud	12
Translated by Michael Perkins	
Three Poems	16
Philip Pardi	
Dead End	20
Melissa Holbrook Pierson	
Three Poems	24
Saul Bennett	
Rooms, Streets, Landscapes, and What We Do There	
In This Place	32
Emily Katz	
Desert...Texas...Film	38
Gerald Seligman	
Three Poems	55
Will Nixon	
Just a Riffle	61
Bob Bachner	
**Love	Crime	Truth	Lies**	
Learning to Jump	76
Minda Zetlin	
Female Troubles	99
Marlene Adelstein	
Ash Wednesday	125
William Boyle	
The Score	139
Alison Sloane Gaylin	

Families: Everybody Has One

Flukenschweilers: Lovely Fire *Paloma J. R. Kopp*	169
Password *Sparrow*	170
Moss *Lorna Smedman*	171
Three Poems *Celia Bland*	177
from Travels With My Aunt *Rachel X. Weissman*	181

Observations. Asides. Epiphanies.

There's One! *Mary Leonard*	188
Seitan's Minion *Richard Klin*	191
Stupidity Wins *Carl Frankel*	194
Fourth of July *Guy Reed*	195

Guilt...Obsession...Mercy...

Bluebeard *Duff Allen*	198
Three Poems *Nancy Rullo*	202
Dierdre Goes On Dancing *Patrick Hyland*	212
Can You Forgive Me, Pumpkin? *Irene McGarrity*	225

Meetings in the Spaces Between

The Cognate Cafe *Isaac Weiner*	232
Six Miniature Fictions *Clark Strand*	238

Contributors 241

Introduction

Stories We Tell Ourselves

A human being is a featherless, storytelling animal.
—Sandor McNab, *The Rebirth of Myth*

Stories fill our lives in the way that water fills the lives of fish. Stories are so all-pervasive that we practically cease to be aware of them.
—Stephen Denning, *The Springboard: How Storytelling Ignites Action in Knowledge-Era Organizations*

The narratives of the world are without number...the narrative is present at all times, in all places, in all societies; the history of narrative begins with the history of mankind; there does not exist, and never has existed, a people without narratives.
—Roland Barthes, *Introduction to the Structural Analysis of the Narrative*

In my first-grade school picture, I'm wearing (along with a crew cut and a toothless grin) a silver police badge, pinned crookedly to my white shirt. Apparently I was "in character," using my imagination to try on a new self like a uniform, creating a narrative about one of my potential futures as an adult.

I had no choice; as a human child, I was simply doing what came naturally: spinning tales through which to understand the world.

That's what *Prima Materia Volume 3* is all about: the ways we create ourselves through stories. When I opened submissions for this issue, I announced the working theme "Necessary Narratives," not so much with an eventual title in mind, but rather to explore my long-standing fascination with the fact that storytelling is woven into the very roots of human nature. Narrative is as essential as food: we simply can't live without it. Whole schools of psychotherapy have grown up around storytelling. It has even been suggested that schizophrenia is essentially the loss of the ability to make a coherent narrative out of one's life.

Neurophilosopher Daniel C. Dennett (in *The Self as Center of Narrative Gravity*) goes further yet. He states that the "self" each of us claims to own is a fiction—an entity that, like an object's center of gravity, is not locatable in the physical world. While the "self" is complex, powerful, and necessary, it nevertheless is made up of nothing more than the stories we tell ourselves and others about who we are.

So what is a "necessary narrative"? Must it be told because it carries some interpersonal, moral, or political message that all people will benefit from? Or must it be told because it benefits the teller, as in the liberation of confession, the empowerment of voicing personal truth? Or is it something more archetypal, more universal, a tale that resonates with something unnamable deep inside each of us, the kind of story that Joseph Campbell might have said originates in the organs of our bodies?

I'm confident you'll find, as I do, that all three of these kinds of stories are present in this collection. Whether the pieces here are ostensibly "truth" or "fiction," whether they are poems, memoirs, personal essays, or traditional short stories, they capture the infinite variety of ways that we "storytelling animals" give narrative structure to our thoughts and lives, and thus create our complex, contradictory, and ultimately magical human selves.

—Brent Robison
January 2004
Mt. Tremper, NY

Endings and Beginnings

Life Full of Light
The Confessions of Arthur Rimbaud

Translated by Michael Perkins

Translator's Note:
This fragment, purporting to be from the hand of the French poet Arthur Rimbaud (1854-1891) was purchased by the translator in a market in Ethiopia some years ago.

<u>Harar, Abyssinia, February, 1891</u>

Because I suspect that I am dying, I have decided to write my confessions. Not to justify myself to a world that means little to me, but to distract myself from the pain and boredom of illness. Writing, which was my first recourse against pain, will be my last refuge from it. We will see how far I get in my race with death.

Because all that we are taught is lies, I am determined that these pages will tell the truth; not pretty, not sentimental, but true as a lion feeding on a gazelle outside the Duke's Gate is true. Whether they will ever be read is no concern of mine. I despise "literature." Writers are hyenas. Those who style themselves modern poets disgust me.

For me, all that matters is freedom, and without truth, there is no freedom. My life, I see now, has been a high rope walk between the two, and I've lost my balance here in this Africa to which I've given my blackened heart. I've lost my freedom. So I will write: now that I cannot travel, I will send words—inadequate words!—traveling across the page to an unknown destination.

My knee is double its normal size. My right leg has given up on me after so much mistreatment. Perhaps it's the syphillis I thought I had beaten, perhaps it's the long miles walked; but I have confined myself to a couch between my desk and the window where I can watch the Freres Magala market and keep track on my servants at their work. What a spectacle! The European traders who call themselves my friends making deals and calling me mad behind my back mix with proud Gallas thin from the famine, the tribeswomen in their white cotton *shammas*. I know them all—what they do, what they say they do, how they struggle to survive. It even seems to me I know their prayers—that I have managed to understand them. I expect that this is a delusion, but I am not crazy.

Since I am immobilized, I must live in my mind, a helpless slave to the *ennui* I have fled all my thirty-six cursed years wandering this earth. I will let memory do the work that once my soul disdained, of focusing on my life. But I repeat my first warning to the faint-hearted: I will not dissemble here. I don't, after all, have enough respect for my fellow beings to make up charitable lies about the events in my own life. I think that I have learned, however begrudgingly, to love our pitiful species, but that doesn't mean I will bow to my own kind's love of euphemism. I am not superior to the lowest specimen of humanity, but if I could, I would rather be a beast than a man. But I was born into the species. I cannot escape it. So much the worse for the jackal who discovers he's a man!

Perhaps if I continue to write in this black ledger, and if it survives—I have asked faithful Djami to bring it to my friend Ras Makonnen, who is goveror of Harar, if I should croak before my sorry-assed, untriumphal return to France and *La Bouche Ombre*, my deadly loving mother—those literary pretenders in Paris will have a good surprise up their noses. Recently I've had a letter from one of them begging me to return to France and "assume the crown of poetry." Piss on that crown of thorns! Give my leg back to me and the gold in my money belt and I'd wander the world to escape such a fatal crowning.

History is a fiction created for the purpose of explaining the inexplicable, so I will write a narrative devoted to explaining the events of a life I cannot explain even to myself. What a joke!

But if there should be a possibility of making money from these confessions, what an even finer and more bitter joke! If I continue to write here, and if it survives my sweat and the Abyssinian sun that scorches the ink from the page, those literary fleas in Paris might one day be presented with a posthumous surprise. My cautionary tale may even light a fire under certain old pals of mind like Paul Verlaine and Germain Nouveau and assorted other grubbers after the laurel.

I can foretell it, the headline in some significant literary review: RIMBAUD FOUND IN AFRICA! Underneath it, some old poems of mine. Perhaps a line from my pals about my sorry circumstances. Thinking of this, I shudder. The only prospect I find pleasing is the idea of Verlaine's ears aflame when he reads these pages. Pages his wife could not destroy. Let him choke on his absinthe. Yes, I would enjoy smelling the surprised shit—across deserts and oceans—in the sissy's pants who proclaimed me dead because I left—him, and our precious Europe, where intelligent worms crawl lazily through empty skulls.

Having failed in so many attempts to make money honestly (as we say here, being *businessmen*, after all) what if after I die this manuscript should bless *La Bouche Ombre* with all the francs she ever dreamed that her poor Arthur would shower on her?

But what does all that matter next to the pain in my leg? *No more poetry*! Let this prose suffice to tell my story. If Europe thinks I am already dead, so much the better! I speak to the next century in these confessions.

Pronouncements will be severe, mostly upon myself. But withhold your pity. I'll tell you some things that will make you wish Azrael had put his hand on me sooner. Now that I know that I will never return to a bourgeois life, I will hold back nothing.

Once that was all I wanted: to return to France with money in my pockets and a Danakil bride on my arm, perhaps to live quietly in Charleville with occasional journeys to places I've dreamed of. Since that is not to be, this is my legacy to my family, my mother and sisters and crazy brother; my modest testament, like my predatory predecessor's Villon.

– *Michael Perkins* –

There will be no American wild west for me, no fabled cannibal isles of the Pacific; Africa has sucked me dry and made me old in the way majestic, ancient Africa does—this miserable, accursed, sublimely beautiful country where I have at last recovered the suffering heart I thought I'd thrown away so long ago, when I believed I was a poet.

Three Poems

Philip Pardi

Flying West

In the seat next to mine sits a big man,
thick-limbed, elbows helplessly ajar
and a baby held every which way

as he works to quiet her. Mother
is in first class (*I insisted*, he explains)
and asking for help would be a terrible defeat.

Baby cries. I look out the window, longing
for mountains, but nothing is possible right now,
there's only this patchwork of need, folding

endlessly in on itself. After forty-one minutes
we're exhausted. Through a gap in the clouds
I see water where there should be terra firma

and I'm certain I'm on the wrong flight,
flying to the wrong city to meet the wrong lover.
The big man sighs, knowing what he must do.

Summoning his courage, an odd air descends
as he begins to sing, his voice soft and shaky
at first, surprisingly treble, but then

encouraged by the newfound quiet,
he closes his eyes, leans into each word
and sings baby and me to sleep.

– *Phillip Pardi* –

Invited to a Party During a Miscarriage

Inexplicably, we decide to go,
the house too small, too large.

We decide to walk. Heading downhill,
I spot my first woodpecker

of the new year, a clumsy red-headed thing
which nearly flies smack

into a maple as it flees us: spring
is here with all its awkward beauty

and colors, furious and brilliant,
hard and unforgiving.

At the party, José takes your hand:
"You look luminous tonight, I can't

quite place my finger on it."
He's right: there's the sheen of

ripened plums in your face,
body blissfully ignorant

of what blood tests have foretold.
We've been here before, you and I,

at times strolling, at times
sprinting from twin thin pink lines

to a finish under cold lights
and as I watch you stir your drink

— Prima Materia —

    with an expression that must look
    to others like happiness

    I'm thinking of the doctor's call
    this afternoon, and the gesture

    you made, oddly baseball-like
    for you, left to right, right

    to left, as you listened
    standing in the kitchen like

    a runner on third, watching
    your team take the field.

– *Phillip Pardi* –

A Boy's Hand

The rule for the woodstove was doors closed
unless you're putting in more wood
and only grown-ups put in more wood
yet there was little Lucas, sitting on his heels,
peering in as if flames were words of joy
and I said nothing. I thought
of what happens to 6 year olds, wondered
if it wasn't happening already,
and said nothing when he reached out
as if to accept a coin.
Behind us there was a scream
but I sat transfixed
as Lucas reached into the woodstove,
bare arm into black cast iron.
From behind us came another shout,
the sudden reconfiguration of furniture,
the tumble of someone trying, failing to get near,
falling, and my name hurled at me such that
I was about to do something — then
the arm withdrawing
and Lucas eyeing his palm with satisfaction.
Reaching down, he let the spider he had saved
crawl from hand to floor
and move on
across the quiet room.

Dead End

Melissa Holbrook Pierson

Yesterday morning the farm boy up at the end of the road was killed. The news, delivered by the young man who had just arrived to start digging post holes with his backhoe, made me feel something very queer right around my duodenum, a concentrated pressing I had never felt before. It was caused by a picture drawing itself quickly in my brain, as by the hand of Walt Disney on old TV, showing how it happened while I slept, with the last breath going out of him right in the appreciable vicinity of my bed pillow. I had been reluctant to face the day; his life went bang. I got up and walked the dogs, fed them breakfast, ate granola while less than a mile up the road frantic disbelief made the sudden scene of disarray surreal. Everything no doubt became strange for them up there, especially time, stretching and retracting in those elastic bands of weirdness that seem to come with their own nauseous soundtrack. One of the last things I had done the night before was exchange waves with him as he drove by in the dusk.

This road is our road. Perhaps we are more proprietary about it because of its dead end, the rocky farm stuffed as far into the hollow as humans and cows could go. Every car that drives past belongs to the road, too, as no one else has much use for it. It goes only to itself.

Last summer, when we first bought the house, I was here alone, airlifted into the middle of home ownership and then dropped, parachute fluttering, into the isolating war zone of a two-hundred-year-old house in which nothing works. I went up to the spring box way behind the barn to attempt to discover why the taps delivered predominantly mud. I found the answer: the box was full of mud. What to do, what to do?

Someone suggested I call the family at the end of the road. They're kind, I was told, and being farmers, full of the practical knowledge that we lose, drop by drop, every time a farm goes under. Soon, I figure, we will know nothing except precisely how long it takes for the plastic window mullions on the six-thousand-square-foot trophy house at Weatherby Farm Estates to start looking like crap.

I called and the father said he would send his son down to look. When he arrived, in a pickup whose rust-to-metal ratio was in exquisite balance, I involuntarily blushed. He was terribly, terribly good-looking. Young, yes. I am married. But I am not dead. He gave me one of the first thrills of immediate attraction I had permitted myself to feel since I got hitched, and it was like taking that first hot shower after emerging from the delirium of flu.

He explained to me that the silt had backed up so high it wasn't letting water enter the box, and he predicted that once it was scooped out, the water would flow in and fill her right up.

Scoop it out?

Could you do it, I asked; I'll pay you fair. (That's how it came out of me, a locution as foreign to me as it undoubtedly was to him.) He smiled a little and said okay, I think I have an old can in the truck. Ten minutes later he was back down, and I gave him thirty dollars, taking a wild guess what "fair" meant. Everyone around these mountains disdains us, the newcomers they call flatlanders, in part because they think we're all rich. My payment notwithstanding, we are about as rich as the average farm family, which is why we bought a two-hundred-year-old house in which nothing works. We might well be thought of as stupid, however.

The next day, both father and son dropped by, leaving mom waiting in the car out front. They wanted to see how I was getting on. I told the boy he was right: the water level had gone right up. Only thing was, now I didn't have any water at all, not even water with mud. The two of them trooped down to the basement and located the water main. Dad said to stand back, and took a wrench and turned. Talking back and forth to each other, as they must have done at every turn on the farm, they used as few words as you can get away with and still communicate something. The water exploded out onto the floor, which is dirt for good reason, and they talked a little more. Dad reached his finger into the pipe and pulled out some gravel and mud, and finally a stone just about the size of the pipe. There's your problem, and then closed it on back up.

Through the rest of the summer, I thought about how I should bake a pound cake and take it up to them.

Now, all day, I think about whether I should go up, should follow the procession of cars that don't belong to our road. As I painted a door, fended off the cat, tried to stay warm on the fifth straight day of cold rain—which is probably what did it to him, trying to load a bulldozer onto the slicked metal of a flatbed—I thought about going up there.

Instead, I took the dogs for a walk in the rain. As we left our immediate yard, we walked past a stone bench engraved with the name of another man who died accidentally, prematurely. Accident. The word itself contains a distant screech of metal crashing. He had lived in this house, and that he died is finally what brought us here, to this road. I had a sudden fright when I saw it—is this place jinxed? Could we, too, be on the road to suffering an accident soon, something that would slam into us out of the mist one rainy day and change us utterly, though we had wanted so badly to stay the same?

When I got back home and changed my wet pants I sat down at the kitchen table. Paralysis had grabbed me by the ankle. I knew I was going to fall face first onto the linoleum if I got up. But perhaps I should bake a coffee cake and take it up the road. Then I realized I was afraid, if I reached for a cookbook, of also finding that my heart had stopped pumping, and that without my blood I would wait at least a week before my husband returned from away and found me, frozen in mid-wonder: Gee, do we have any butter? I stayed sitting, my fingers playing with the paper clip and penny that lay on the edge of the table. Darkness fell from the roof past the windows.

My mind got up without me and started up the road, not even taking a flashlight. It heard the sound of rushing water everywhere. It knew where to turn, and in the darkness a kind of second sight came to it. Everything became visible. Only at the dead end did it stop in perplexity, because it had never been all the way there before.

Three Poems

Saul Bennett

The Bitter Riches Of Chocolate

Chocolate bars, you surely will recall, were short for all
save soldiers, sailors, etc., and when they showed up in shops
disappeared quicker than The Shadow dissolved on the radio,
or more often never appeared, owners holding them off shelves,
back-rooming them instead at unpatriotic prices. A nickel Hershey's, say,
larger than today's 60¢ size, could command 12 or, even, outrageously,
15 cents, but all those civilians busy black-marketing similar exotica
were untroubled by such prices, as they were gouging back. If you could
turn up nylons, or penny-into-dime Fleer's Double Bubble,
your unborn grandchildren were a lock for college paid in full.

My father was a surgical glass salesman then, working hospitals and labs
from Manhattan up through Bridgeport and New Haven. Since you couldn't
eat or wear his items, you say, why is my father in this poem?
Just starting out, he was "nephewed" by a doting older customer
who also imported microscopes, some Swiss line, German-sounding,
and a surprising number of fathers seemed in need then of better
microscopes for sons, nephews, whomever, don't ask me why,
though having something to do with medical school when the War ended.
You expected to pay, even at wholesale, had one been available, a couple
thousand times more for a superb microscope than for a Baby Ruth
or Clark bar—so sniff the delicious possibilities: my father picks one up,
say, for a hundred, and turns it around for a deuce. But when he could
get the things, and talk of his touch went way past Sunnyside,
where we lived, out as far as Rego Park and Forest Hills, he was happy

to oblige at not even a bubble gum hunk more than his cost. I once
overheard a certain Mr. Ed Napp, the two-chins candy wholesaler father
of my friend Freddy across the block, egging my father he was coconuts
to trade a dollar for only a hundred cents, but all my father could do
was shrug, a little embarrassed, maybe, he lacked sharks' teeth.
About 20 years later—less—in his young 30s, Freddy picked up
cancer and died. Afterward, observing Mr. Napp, who'd made such
a killing off his bars he never worked again, you saw in all seasons
but winter a pot-belly-in-a-white-T-shirt-Beefeater, short a shave,
planted at a slumped attention in front of his apartment house; who might,
when hailed, nod, but never speak, ever. Superstitious always, I felt
my father had strung out my life by shooting straight in the War,
keeping me alive all these years, so far past the end of my own child, 24.

– *Prima Materia* –

After The Last Cheyenne Left Harlem

I n Harlem, for a quarter, my mother baby-sat summers in the heat
of the Coolidge years for the Zipes daughters, Elaine and Flossie,
whose mother Rose's knuckle nose, coal-brewed eyes and clumpy black
braids reminded her children of the Cheyenne brave on a '24 nickel.

Only a dime or so older than the Zipes girls, Mother was branded "Schnookie"
by Rose, whose accountant husband skipped the Harlem-to-the-Bronx interregnum,
sailing them straight across the East River to the New World—Astoria, in Queens,
where my father took me years later, at 6, in FDR's third, to Flossie's wedding

reception at Rose's home. Scores swayed across a 2-family-attached ocean
of rooms drowning warmed salty cashews with apricot and blackberry
schnapps before wetting themselves good in creamy herring pools
with onions. In the kitchen later, alone with me, my father, rarely in his life

addressing drink but adoring sweets always, I watched remove chunk
after chunk of break-up dark chocolate with raisins and nuts from a
brown paper sack larger, even, than my scarlet-fevered infant sister
Schnookie was sitting for at home. Why I conjure now, who knows, Schnookie

mending an ailing child in that nice-light 2-bedroom over a
third cup of Holland House drip, swallowing all-ears the happy shouts
a mile away "Guh'bye! Guh'bye!" poured by guests on the departing bride,
at 24 the age of Schnookie's grandddaughter, my first child, at death?

— *Saul Bennett* —

Among The Few Who Didn't Make It Out To Gatsby's Party On His Lawn In West Egg That Memorable Summer Evening In 1922 (Chapter IV)

From somewhere in Jersey, then, came Jimmy Geffen, whom my father
      knew from business and supposed a hidden Jew.
He came in right after Slice Joost,
As did tall old proper Mr. Popper, Father's early mentor
    in surgical glass sales, widowed now and though practically
    November splendid in a spiny sort of way
    all in seersucker beneath hair cotton-white;

From Mother's side there came the Halpern girls,
    second cousins past 50—called girls
    within the family as they had not yet married;
Mother's all-bones young aunt Fannie Flam and husband
    August, said to never say a word and who ate
    off Fannie's plate with his only hand.

From Great Neck—West Egg itself!—
    —Mother's struck-it-rich-in-resins cousin
    Lew Pakula and his stuck-up shrimpy wife Bella,
    last in, first out and not until December coughing up
    a chemistry set with a cheesy microscope.

From Father's native Astoria to begin, his widowed father,
    recounting over handfuls of chick peas he shook
    before downing, as if readying to roll craps,
    the "Blizzard of '88" (he was 12)
    and of having slipped every November
    into his palm by a Tammany hack on Steinway Street
    a buck to vote Demo at 3 or 4 hour intervals;

– Prima Materia –

The bloated Doc Feuerstein, who delivered me hard
        by Penn Station at the late French Hospital on West 30th;
Seymour Fain, an Errol Flynn double but handsomer, and his stunning wife,
        Ella, a Gene Tierney ringer but sultrier (they never had children).
        Seymour had some vague connection
        with the movies, handing out passes for the Roxy
        and the Capitol on Broadway near the old Garden on 50th
        whenever he came around to play gin;
Gerard (Slice) Joost from down near under, still,
        Hell Gate Bridge, hooking up
        with Father in '25 to grab the Northwest Queens
        Mens' Handball Doubles crown, his nickname a bow
        to the peerless spin he was said to have put on the black ball.
        Slice arrived in lilac slacks and some sort of—cutaway
        boasting a carnation dyed Blarney green
        shot from a lapel the length of Delaware.
        Slice came to everything, with someone new
        on his arm each time and was always last to leave.

From New York came the Buxbaum Brothers, N.S. and Irwin,
        who sold trusses and a little surgical glass (provided by Father)
        out of a shop under the El on Third across from Bloomingdale's;
The courtly E.M. Suder, head of Father's firm, dropped
        by a chromium-loaded black Packard, make and model
        Jerome Korn said he adored enough to want
        to snatch to celebrate his next birthday.

From out on Long Island came someone's
        Uncle Nehemiah Somebody, so religious, it was said,
        he had allowed his wife to be driven
        home without him from the hospital with
        new twins, as they'd bounced her on
        a sabbath Saturday, when motoring was proscribed.

– *Saul Bennett* –

    (He'd been brought from Long Beach
    by a nephew before sundown Friday
    and put him up overnight with the beadle.)

Touching friends from the apartments on either side,
Bennett Ostrove, whose remarkable slow-breaking stuff later took him
    as high as Scranton in the mid-Minors before his mother
    telephoned as he hit the mound one evening in Elmira
    ordering him through the clubhouse boy
    to get home finally for accounting studies nights
    and "work normal" days. Four nights later
    in Wilkes-Barre, pasted good in the 2nd,
    Bennett took the midnight bus home forever.
Jerome Korn, who 6 or 7 years later suffered
    a stretch inside the Ft. Riley, Kansas, stockade
    upon hunting out (after 6 or 7 PX beers, he allowed),
    and breaking the nose of, an artillery sergeant-instructor,
    advancing after a discharge Other Than Honorable
    to armed robbery at fake gun point of the Sinclair station
    on Skillman Avenue, thusly earning
    fairly serious penitentiary time (or, as Mrs. Korn put Jerome's
    absence to new tenants, "away at a nice college out-of-town").

Of my parents' friends from our floor, Fran & Dot O'Horn,
    scrapping always, and later divorced;
the Bohigians, importing currants, nutmeats and cigars, Mr.'s grift.
    (I never knew his first name—Aram, or Haig, maybe.)

Our super, of course, Mr. Langenbrunner, and his trusty
    busty wife, Mary Pat, whispered by some of the fathers to be
    the sister of the often-quoted-in-the-tabloids Ned Bresnahan,
    promotions chief for the baseball Giants
    back in '33, their next-to-last World Series winner in New York;

– Prima Materia –

That scrumptious upswept dusky-blonde with glistening
        shivery legs, Miss Christine Majeski, Father's secretary,
           looking lost let off by her parents from nearby Maspeth;
Archer Miles (née Asa Milstein, my uncle mentioned some years later),
        a wild card, uninvited, late arriving, Mother's
        bespectacled redheaded younger brother's
        private dick pal, packing heat,
        you could see, underneath a robin's-egg-blue
        double-breasted suit jacket that looked to be
        at war with aqua slacks . On his arm,
        a certain "Miss Clay" (Klee? Cullay?),
        introduced as his, well, his fiancee.

All these and more came to my bar-mitzvah in the fall.

Rooms, Streets, Landscapes... and What We Do There

In This Place

Emily Katz

Sometimes she purrs like there is a motor in her chest. I'll turn on the television, or turn out the light and begin to drift off to sleep, when there is a loud and deep fluttering in the side of my ear, right where the low tones hit. She wants attention, maybe she misses the woman who lives in this house but has gone to another state to sit with her father, sick in the hospital. Usually when I run my hand along her multicolored back to the tip of her tail she purrs louder. Occasionally she'll bat my hand away, or move to the other side of the bed.

   This is how I begin: Every so often I'll forget where I am, whose house I am in. I will look out the window and into the street, and I'll recognize a small town in upstate New York, the narrowness of the roads and the closeness of houses in condensed neighborhoods that branch off from the main street in town. I don't know anyone in the area except one or two distant acquaintances, so I've chosen this summer to be completely alone besides these two cats I'm watching over. It's been five days since I got here and I have only walked down the main street once. I'm certain that the townspeople who sit on their front porches or carry their mail while walking two dogs at a time know I'm just house-sitting, that I'm not really one of them. I stay close to the house, and if I leave I go for miles. My cousin, who is constantly analyzing our behaviors and patterns, told me yesterday that he noticed our family has no moderation, we go all or nothing. I will sit on the front porch, or the back stoop, or safely indoors, or I will drive into open country miles away. The things in between make me a little nervous, like the talkative neighbors who sit on their front porch and play guitar in the evenings because they live in that house attached to the porch, and I am just here temporarily.

– Emily Katz –

I'm convinced that we in this house pretend to be peaceful, but really we are temperamental and maybe even a bit confused. There are two cats and I here for the next month and a half, and even though we appreciate each other's company we are all missing someone, and something is missing. Every so often the cats will bat at my hand, or run away when I invite them to sit close to me, and every so often something will pull at me hard. I'll wish for another human body, and they'll wish for the woman they know and love to appear outside the window they stare out in the afternoons.

For now we have each other, and I have an immense amount of space to do whatever I want to do, only I don't know yet what will fill it. The first night I was here I felt everything close in on me, and I walked out to the front stoop and sat there to remind myself of space, and of openness. Of the possibilities of a productive summer, of solitude in a constructive way. Of sunny mornings waking up with two cats curled around my head, of nights that will end up eventually in the same way. They come upstairs separate of each other, after I've already gotten into bed, but when I turn in my sleep I can feel them there, warm and soft beside me.

While I am here there are three bookshelves of books I want to read, and it's been five days and I have almost finished my second novel. It is vaguely about water, about kinds of water that drown us and about the kinds that don't, and even though I concentrate on the words, sometimes when I am reading I feel the hard tug, the inside of my chest drop down. If someone could teach me how not to miss, how to accept who may be there and not there at any given time, I could live without distraction. I wouldn't have to zero in on every line that reminded me of someone, or every passage that captured the despair I am trying so hard to keep down deep, to not look at in the face. I would not look at the words but really drift off, thinking of another body beside mine, or in the chair facing me on the opposite side of the living room. I would not have to look out the window so much, because I would believe so much more easily that I am here alone, that I am doing this now.

This woman's house is littered with pieces of her: she proves to me she is a writer by leaving pens everywhere, by having unopened packages of expensive-looking ones just inside her desk drawer that I open to look for a stamp, of which she has dozens; a letter writer too I'm sure. She has a computer with thousands of written documents on it in a quiet study that has piles of papers neatly stacked on the floor. There is spinach fettuccini in the pantry, and a bottle of wine in the refrigerator. She has an empty Corona box, and an almost empty six-pack of ginger ale which I finish off my first night here. Her bathroom has minty-smelling hand salves and sweet-smelling face lotions and toners, and her bedroom is bare except for an antique rocking chair from a distant relative of hers, a television set, and a double bed covered in a white bedspread and light sheets. The walls are pale green; I remember the day she painted them because I was here the evening after, and it reminds me of summer. It is summer, and I am living here instead of her. The cats are always scratching me to wake up so they can eat in the morning, and there is a specific procedure to putting out the trash that I forget now that it's the night to put it out. I miss people I told myself I wouldn't miss like this, and there is a pushing and a pulling that sometimes wafts away into the air when I feel myself rising up, when I realize in some moments that I am happy here with this peacefulness, and these cats.

The kinds of water that do not: It has been raining for three days now, and something inside of me has settled more comfortably. I'm not afraid to turn up the stereo and drown myself to make things more exciting, and it scatters my thinking while it's on. I've been here another week, and even though I tell myself I'm not counting because I'm not exactly sure what I'm counting toward, that is one less week of time to go through. The woman whose house I am staying in called me this morning to tell me of a spreading cancer, of a summer of chemotherapy, but she still had the calmness that always reigns through her speech, and when the cats came into the room I told them she was doing all right. Her telephone has become something to ground me: I receive one call a day, most often from the same person, a friend who is staying back home in Syracuse this summer, and her phone call separates my day into parts. If she calls in the evening I will most likely drive to the video store I like, forty minutes away, when the conversation is over, her voice still buzzing in my head for the duration because it's the only communication I can really count on here. If she calls earlier, then I start my day over when we hang up—I'll abandon old projects and begin new ones, and I'll be remotivated, or maybe just trying to keep myself busy because I know there probably won't be another phone call today, that mine and hers was the only conversation to happen for awhile.

    I have to remind myself sometimes that I chose to be alone, and this isn't a burden placed on me. A different friend writes me a letter that says he craves the simplicity of my life right now. When we talk every so often he asks me what I made myself for dinner last night, what I did when I woke up this morning, where I stopped when I went for my afternoon drive through the Catskills. I tell him I got lost on the winding roads that cover this area, and he gets jealous when I tell him I used the Hudson and the mountains behind it to find my way home. He craves the quietness of this house, this space around me, and by now I have already begun to take this for granted. I crave the companionship he has of old friends each night, but I know if I had this it wouldn't be enough. I would want more space for aloneness, more time to write, less talking and commotion around me. Less of hearing the same things from the same people, but listening anyway because there is nothing else to focus on; the things around me would be the same things I have seen all my life, the same things I've convinced myself I am sick of.

    I am reminded of where I would be instead of here, and I am satisfied; I am reminded of perpetual silence and solitude when I open my eyes each morning, and I wish for something more. The hum of the refrigerator, the fact that each item is exactly where I placed it the night before, and no one but me will be the one to move it. When I sit down to write I want to keep at it until I've got every moment recorded, everything here as if I am just an observer of this peaceful and solitary life, but I stop writing after a certain point because I am afraid of ruining something, maybe of going too far. The same reason I decide, At the next town I will turn around, when I am out driving far and unfamiliar roads and I have time and space enough for complete freedom. I pull onto a side road when I see an old wooden sign for Fleishmanns, I fill up my gas tank at the oldest filling station I've ever seen and buy a pack of antiquated gum for my ride home. I turn around, I go back to the cats, to my vegetable dinners and the American Movie Classics I've taken to watching.

And I've got this new thing under my belt: I am living alone. I am not just house-sitting, or cat sitting, but I am living alone in this house, and this could be my house in which I live alone. My friend says she's proud of me for not living under my parents' roof for the entire second summer of college, that I have this month and a half of some kind of adulthood now. I cook healthy meals, I water plants and wash dishes, I lock the doors each night and turn out all the lights. I walk to the post office each day to check the P.O. box, I read books by now deceased men and women in the blue easy chair in the living room each night, often with a cat draped across my lap. And I feel satisfied with these scenes; if I could take pictures of my life here those would be them, and I would send them to everybody: Look how grownup and peaceful I am. But there are the other scenes, the ones where I look for a part-time job to fill my time half-heartedly, where I walk around the house unsettled because I miss people and human touch, or looking at someone else's eyes besides the cats. The ones where I watch reruns of old sitcoms because I am bored, or eat Oreos because I don't feel like making anything else. The ones where I am reaching so hard for something that isn't really within my reach, and something I can't place my finger on but I know it's necessary for me to be able to breathe better, in this air, in this place.

    For now: I think about how it's easier to get excited about things when I do them by myself. I think about what it means to not have to try to get along with someone so nobody is getting hurt, and what kinds of thoughts about solitude and introspection can come out of this summer. How sometimes these thoughts make me nervous but they can also be good, like when I feel maybe I am dependent on someone that it is dangerous for me to be dependent on; I remind myself that here I am the caretaker of these cats and this home instead of the one being taken care of by friends and family, and that this way can feel like love and acceptance too. I think about how I sat in this same kitchen a month ago with a group of writers and one of them shared with us her thoughts on space and time and sound, and because of the way she spoke with evenness and breathing room I felt at ease, like I could think in this kitchen with her space later on, when I was alone. How she reassures me and reassures herself with the words, "Okay, you are doing this now," and in her writing asks open-ended questions like, "What do you do?" I think about what it means that I always get to listen to the music I want to exactly when I want to, and how I can appreciate a phone call or a visit more than I could a month ago. I think about how I am learning the rhythms of my thoughts inside my head, and how often these rises and falls are not only expected, but also a comfort. I think about how I can take showers with the door open. And things like what it means that I am the only one in this house and the cats will turn to me when they want food or love, or when the orange one is searching for a forehead to put his sleepy fuzzy one against while we sleep, because last night he curled up so close to me, he did this.

Desert...Texas...Film

Gerald Seligman

For nearly two days the train rocked through the lush bayous of southern Louisiana. Dense green kudzu smothered trees in a landscape returned to the primeval. Even with eyes closed, I saw endless vines and leaves and scum-covered swamps. I drifted off. When I awoke, I snapped up in my seat. Suddenly everywhere was desert. Patches of cactus lay in sand-strangled terrain. Where was all the green? How does nature do this? We had entered southwestern Texas.

There was grandeur in the miles of open, parched wilderness, the extended vistas, the one-lane roads stretching into the distance, but as we swept into El Paso, the majesty vanished. The poorer sections of town looked like squatter's camps cast in concrete. These and warehouses and sprawling flat factories stretched their somber greeting miles before the city center. I almost regretted having to get off here, but was looking forward to seeing a friend, Martin Gressmann, who was on location for a German film shoot.

With the first step off the train, the heat sucked the sweat right out of me, drenching my shirt in an instant. I balled up the light sweater I wore as protection from the train's air-conditioning and stuffed it into my bag. The station, a red brick model cast from the classic mold, was still under construction, and as I dodged the debris, a fellow I'd been trading stories with hailed out a last good-bye. I turned, waved and tumbled over a pile of cinder blocks. It hurt so much I sprang up to deny it, but glanced down to see gravel-pocked blood on both arms and a leg.

I limped into El Paso, my bag slung over my shoulder, heading for the towering sign of the Hotel Plaza. Oceanic waves of heat rose from the pavement, smothering this city of perpetual glare. My eyes squinted through narrow slits between lashes. "Why here?" I asked aloud. From the hotel lobby I rang Martin.

He was already on his way down in the elevator balancing dollies laden with huge cameras, banged-up metal cases and bulky film equipment. Martin was harried, and we hardly exchanged greetings before I checked into a costly room, hurled my bags onto the bed, and rushed into the waiting van to be whisked off to the desert set. Driving was Mark Milner, the stills photographer. I marveled. Just one week before, I'd been home in New York. Bored.

At 6 p.m. it was still 100 degrees. Sitting on a wooden slat in front of paint-chipped gas pumps, I picked the grit from my scratches. Cars were lined up beside me, but the pumps were dry. And though the sign behind read A-1 Diner, no food was served and the cupboards were bare. The attached shanty, a two-room excuse for home, led out to the rusted wrecks of cars that faced a dilapidated, whitewashed billboard used as a giant movie screen. It seemed like some post-apocalyptic drive-in.

Built only two weeks before, the blistered settlement was a German designer's view of an American scene informed by American films for a future German audience. Cars pulled over, and their drivers tipped back broad-brimmed hats and scratched their foreheads. "Funny, I never noticed the place before, and I been passin' this way *for years*." When friendly replies hailed back through thick German accents they were really stumped.

Beyond us clay-colored sand stretched out infinitely, while the parched air belied any sense of distance. Mountains sixty or more miles beyond looked close enough to be within an hour's stroll. Telephone poles shrank into the horizon where flat-bottomed clouds billowed upwards like white cotton candy.

"This is all Army land, the Fort Bliss Missile Testing Range," Milner said. He was one of the few Americans on the crew. Slim, with bloodshot blue eyes and cropped blond hair, he had a thin, braided strand of ponytail wagging below his shoulder blades. He offered background and filled me in on what I'd missed.

"One day there were three soldiers out on one of those week-long survival maneuvers. They stopped by to visit us. They were supposed to stay out of sight of the troops who were searching all over trying to find them. We'd have to stop shooting all the time because a helicopter would be hovering just overhead, or a tank platoon would come racing past at sixty miles per hour. Those guys were crazy. One of them caught a rattlesnake. They cooked it and ate it—survival, you know," he said, with a smile. "Though they sure liked our catered meals, so they joined us. They spent the whole day hiding out in the whorehouse we built." He pointed to it, a purple, wooden shack just off the dirt road adjoining the highway. "Finally some trucks pulled up and all these soldiers hopped out. One fired his gun into the air... I don't know why. They looked all over the place, but couldn't find them anywhere. They didn't think to look in the whorehouse—and where else would a soldier be?"

The crew was setting up for the day's shoot. Martin, who was assistant to the cinematographer, was in the open truck, shielded from a sun still bright at this late hour. After cleaning the Arriflex, he plunged his arms into long black sleeves to load the film magazines. As members of the crew approached, he'd call out introductions. This was a crew who'd worked on many of the most accomplished films of the German cinema revival of the 1970s, with directors like Rainer Fassbinder, Werner Herzog, and Wim Wenders. The cinematographer Martin Shäfer shot Wenders' famed *Kings of the Road*. Shäfer was wearing scuffed cowboy boots and a green khaki jumpsuit. Strapped around his waist was a rawhide belt and brass buckle that read "Marty." He rarely talked and chain-smoked unfiltered cigarettes. "The German film industry would be nowhere without cigarettes," an electrician declared.

Set-up established a pace that hardly wavered. I had only been in El Paso an hour and a half, with the train's lilting progress replaced by this sluggish temporal crawl. I didn't know what to do with my excitement—everyone looked so bored—so I took a few deep breaths and tried to slow down to match their rhythm.

With an hour or more passing in such preparation, I did begin to calm down. And knowing a film was in progress, having nothing whatsoever to do, finally even relaxed me. Within a few hours, staring off into the distance, I actually forgot why we were there, until a violent, crazed scream ripped through the house. "Incest scene," Heidi Kirsch said when I jumped. I hadn't even known they'd started filming. Then, three or four times in succession came the same scream, the same sound of furniture toppling onto the floor, of bodies slammed into a wall—"Cut! We'll try it again."

First scene of the day and already eyes rolled and knowing sighs were exchanged. The crew didn't seem too enthusiastic. I asked to see a script. Like many German films of American life this one ends apocalyptically. The shooting schedule:

Day 30: The tower falls down.

Day 31: Johnny's truck drives into diner.

Day 32: The diner blows up.

For the synopsis the director Vadim Glowna wrote: "It is about passions. Suffering. Eroticism. Brutality. Insanity. About dignity, death and waiting. About heat. And about music." That should about cover it, I thought. "Visually, the style is reminiscent of Diane Arbus and Walker Evans." Originally entitled *This Rigorous Life*, it was changed along the way to *Nothing Left to Lose*. Somehow the script didn't reveal very much, so I asked the soundman Martin Muelter for the details. "German immigrants, bad luck," he replied.

The male lead was Jerzy Radziwilowicz, star of Andrzej Wajda's seminal films of Poland's Solidarity years, *Man of Marble* and *Man of Iron*. The same intensity that filled the screen stared out at an actual meeting. But Jerzy stayed off by himself mostly, always reading a crumpled paperback, or sitting quietly, staring into the sand with his head resting on his forearms.

Of all the crew, Heidi Kirsch was friendliest. The way she shook my hand and smiled warmly allayed any fears I had of intruding. Perhaps I was a curiosity: Why come voluntarily? As she disinfected my cuts I asked about her other film work. She mentioned Fassbinder's *Despair*.

"Yeah," I said with a sigh. "I was so sorry to hear of Fassbinder's passing." This was 1982 and it was still a recent event.

"It was to be expected," she replied brusquely. "He drank too much, smoked too much, never slept, always did drugs—nobody can live long like that." Her voice betrayed her sorrow. I asked about Dirk Bogarde. Her eyes opened wide, and she ran over to her make-up kit to fetch a Polaroid. It showed Bogarde, despairing indeed, with a full week's stubble of beard. "It's the only picture from a job that I carry," she said after staring at it intently. Handing it over reluctantly, she added, "He was such a darling, so professional. No one ever had to go searching for *him* when it was time for a scene." I wondered who they did have to search for.

"He plays to perfection that very British kind of coolness, that detachment. Is that how he is off the screen, too?"

"Oh, no, he's not at all distant. He was so kind." She took the picture back to look again. Her voice dropped to a whisper. "I really fell in love with him. The only problem is, well..." Her voice trailed off, and she stared at the photograph for awhile. I rolled down the leg of my pants and thanked her.

As the sun sank over a distant ridge, swiftly passing clouds cast drops of rain and then moved on. I grabbed an iced beer that Udo, the production assistant, religiously kept stocked. He had a physique that revealed an absolutely Bavarian appreciation for the stuff.

I walked into the house, where Vera was acting the transitional scene of her sprint to insanity. Let's see if I can get this straight. In the film, Joseph, a happily married man played by Radziwilowicz, goes to jail after killing the man who raped his sister, played here by Vera. A jail scene shot on location in El Paso purportedly featured a spaghetti riot. When Joseph returns after five long years, in one of those coincidences even cinema struggles under, he arrives during his mother's funeral. Vera, he soon discovers, converses with herself regularly, and, to make matters worse, doing so keeps her from the many tasks of the family's calling: pumping gas, flipping eggs in the diner, and running films at the adjacent drive-in. It all falls to Joseph, who—well, to be frank, here I did get a bit lost, but it seems that Joseph somehow managed to have misplaced his wife in the interim and is himself showing signs of growing derangement as he tries to keep the whole shebang going.

Watching the unwieldy scene reel off into successive takes, I thought: but at least he's convincing. Vera, though she was portraying a simple-minded country girl gone simpler still, looked like she'd be more at home discussing current events in a café. And as for acting, she tendered the grandest, most sweeping dramatic gestures as if they were semaphores to peg an emotion at a distance of two hundred yards. Like a silent screen actress, fear brought soul-shaking shivers; distraction a long, vacant look into the distance; and sorrow the back of a hand smacked to her brow with a sigh. In close-up that slap would send members of the audience tumbling backwards into the last rows of the theater. When I stared, awe-struck, I was nudged. "Director's wife," someone whispered.

Vera was standing by the window in a tattered nightgown. She mumbled atmospherically, subtle as a high school starlet, then glided from the window past candles set on the floor, of all places. Her gown was to catch fire, prompting Jerzy to put it out with his hands. His hands were to catch fire, too. Jerzy didn't much like the idea.

"Now don't worry," assured Harry Wiesenhaan, one of two special effects experts as he brushed the flammable gel onto Jerzy's hands. "It burns for a few seconds without pain and is easily extinguished." He had a harelip and the metallic edge to his voice common to the condition. With each ill-fated take, more gel was applied. Jerzy looked at his hands and the rest of us looked at each other with mounting concern.

"Don't worry," Ben, the other effects man, echoed. "It's good for the skin." Though he was serious, all laughed riotously.

These two Dutchmen, the stills photographer Milner later told me, were the Laurel and Hardy of special effects; they even had the memorable physical contrasts. Harry was short and agreeably plump, while Ben was long and lean. Both loved their jobs and talked with maniacal gleams in their eyes of blowing the place up a few weeks hence. It was clear that here were two men in the admirable position of having found their ideal vocations. I could easily imagine them as children, derailing model trains in monumental mishaps and decapitating their sister's dolls.

Vera, meanwhile, hovered by the window, by the candles —"Cut! Take three." By the window—"Cut! Take four." By the window again.

The heat was stifling. Before each take, the prop girl launched glittering, metallic dust from a towel, giving the heat its visual counterpart. The light from thirty or more candles— snuffed out and re-lit for each take—was caught in their shiny fluttering surfaces. Glitter landed everywhere, sticking to beads of sweat, and coursing down necks in glistening rivulets.

Without warning a cloudburst thundered over us, and everyone paused wordlessly and stared, transfixed. I walked over to the window. The desert sand greedily drank every drop of a fierce downpour that would easily have flooded any other terrain. A heavy theatrical light just outside the window crashed down by the sheer force of the wind. A door banged open and the rain drenched a section of floorboards in seconds. Yet no one moved. For the entire half-hour of torrential rain, not a word was spoken.

The rain just as suddenly stopped, and Vera returned to her post by the window. I stepped outside and strolled off. Watching the crew, particularly on a set slowed by the stifling heat of the desert, it's hard to imagine how anything gets done.

The cloudburst had crossed the road and was drenching a mile-wide lane of sand. As it swept like a veil over the desert, the rain turned violet in the dimming sunset, gathered in by a sky of gold, burnt sienna, and deep red.

Two flushed-out rattlesnakes sidled away from me, leaving a swirling trail of S's, and there was one still tarantula, dead. The moon peeked over a distant ridge, rising full over the landscape. I turned and noticed others watching too—"Hey!

You're in the frame!" I hastened over to the purple whorehouse, Open 24 Hours.

Standing, pissing in the sand, was a tall man in a knit shirt whom I hadn't seen before. He was Dieter Flimm, the set designer. He related the myriad difficulties they'd encountered scouting the right location and then building the set. It was his first project outside of theater.

"It's incredibly well done," I enthused, and then tossed off insensitively, "I should think it'll be difficult for you when they blow it all up."

He shook his head gravely.

He asked if I'd ever been in the desert before, so I related an experience that morning—only that morning?—on the train. This was indeed my first time, but the wide expanses, the dry, jagged hills, the boulders and crags had all seemed so familiar. A man next to me had said it first. "I just can't help it. My only connection with any of this is through the movies." He was from North Carolina and had a stamp of perpetual bewilderment fixed on his wide brow. "I keep expecting to see cowboys and Indians whooping it up out there. They seem like they're missing, somehow."

Throughout the observation car rang the same comments. One parrot-faced fellow was convinced the ghost of John Wayne rode the ghost of a horse out there just beyond our line of sight. I wondered if this sense of emptiness came from the desert itself or from the absence of war parties and covered wagons ringed in protective circles. The familiarity had comforted us all somehow. It lent the scene a greater impact simply because we'd all seen it in the movies since we were kids.

"So to be here, in fact," I said to Dieter, "is actually a bit disorienting—though this *is* a film set," I added with a laugh, "so that's a compromise at least."

"I've hardly had time to realize where I am," he said. "There's so much last-minute design and construction. I'll probably be back in Germany at my desk, and then I'll suddenly say, 'Oh yeah, look where I was.'"

I walked back, eyes downcast for each snake-watching step, and then sat in a chair for a long while. Bolts of silent lightning shot from clouds, momentarily illuminating patches of sky before returning them to the deepest black. One at a time, crew members would walk off by themselves, gaze out, then return and sit down again. I filled a pipe with tobacco and drew on it peacefully. Everything was so very still, even the occasional car whisking down the highway did little to interrupt the enveloping silence. Occasionally a bird would wing frantically from a tangle of bushes, but then there'd be quiet again. Even my thoughts stopped whirring about. Looking off at the moon that had risen high into the evening, I blew smoke rings to lasso it.

Then, Udo, his fat belly bouncing, shot towards us shouting urgently in German. Chairs were emptied as everyone leapt to their feet in confusion. Udo yanked up a heavy end of the water cooler and summoned help to carry it out front where a military pick-up truck idled by the empty pumps. Inside was a skin-and-bones blond kid folded into himself, unconscious. The Army MP was slapping him in the face rhythmically, saying in a dull monotone, "Come on, come on, get up, wake up, come on." Nothing doing. The kid lay still, limply tucked between the door and seat. I had so thoroughly adapted to the surreal pace and spectacle of the shooting that I could only view the unfolding scene in terms of its dramatic content.

"What happened?" Heidi asked.

"Blow out," the MP reported. "Went off the road." He looked up at us expectantly, needing something, a command, anything. He sensed Udo was in charge. Udo splashed water from the cooler into the kid's face. He momentarily came to, then slumped back down again. "You'd better get him to the hospital," Udo said.

"Yessir," snapped the MP, glad for an order. He drove off saying he'd report back to us.

"That's the guy who watches over the set when we leave," Heidi said.

By the end of that first night, all the moths that had fluttered too close to the floodlights had spun wildly on the ground and died, joining a wide circle of dead insects and black beetles an inch thick.

As we drove back to El Paso, Udo noticed the kid's car ditched in the sand. He pulled over. Two stark skids curved abruptly off the pavement, then there was the car itself ten feet down and facing the wrong way. Between the car and skid was nothing. It must have been airborne. Udo scurried back and forth, laughing loudly.

An hour into the next day's shooting, I felt as if I hadn't even slept in the hotel. In the house, Jerzy lifted Vera into his arms and threw her onto the creaking bed. His brow was caked with fake blood. She flailed her arms wildly, screaming. They fought, he slapped her, her arms reached around his neck, calm, a kiss. "Okay, one more rehearsal." It was still the incest scene. But where did the blood come from? So far as I knew, all he'd done since the day before was extinguish her gown. I stepped out and sighed.

A car drove up to the pumps. "There's no gas here," I told the driver, then noticed it was the kid from the night before. He was beaming, and everyone raced up to fire questions.

"I was drunk," he replied proudly, with a wide smile that wrinkled the skin of his flat face and narrowed his bright little eyes.

"But what happened?"

"Tried to fly."

I re-entered the house to Vera's crying and sat down on a metal camera case, inexplicably drained and exhausted. I soon fell asleep, woke with a start, and went back outside again.

We ate a catered meal under a full moon on tables and chairs dug into the sand. The special effects men entertained.

During breaks I often approached Radziwilowicz with the intention of striking up conversation, but would halt a few paces off and turn elsewhere. There was a distance he maintained that I feared crossing. It was a time when I measured myself by the people I encountered, so I had to keep vigilant. I kept framing questions like "Are you able to work in Poland?" "Is Wajda still in the country?" "What happened to the Film Polski unit?" This was years before the end of Communism, after all, with Poland still under martial law. But each question seemed like it would be an inexcusable violation of privacy. Though I did once ask him to pass a napkin, which he did, and when Heidi applied another fantastically realistic wound to Jerzy's brow, I observed, "She heals my wounds and opens yours."

After dinner the shooting moved outside to the gas pumps. They'd hired a local named Rudy to play the role of "Beatnik," who'd come roaring into the gas station on a motorcycle. I never before associated beatniks and bikes, and when he arrived, his slicked black hair and greasy beard, his sleeveless black T-shirt, angry biceps and rock-hard beer belly ejected him for all time from a Greenwich Village coffee house.

The camera was mounted on a track and the scene began with Rudy pumping his own gas. Jerzy, by now at least as deranged as his sister, ran by with his shirt flapping and his thoughts, as it were, elsewhere. "Hey, man!" Rudy yelled, "What kind of a place is this? I been waitin' here all day!"

"Why don't you just shut up and get out of here!" Jerzy stammered, and kept running.

"Hey, no one talks to me that way! Get back here, you punk!" Rudy leaped on his bike, revved it to a roaring start and raced after him, but Jerzy had already shimmied up the drive-in's projector tower. "I'll be back for you, you son of a bitch!" shouted Rudy, and off he zoomed.

Rudy was a hit. The set, which had frozen during the take, now bristled with cheers and patted backs. Marijan, the assistant director, gave the thumbs-up, and Vadim Glowna, snapped out of the malaise of endless details, grinned from ear to ear. Here the film's perception of an ever-present violence lurking beneath the American surface became flesh in their beatnik from El Paso.

The shot was repeated four more times, each one better than the last. Heidi kept applying sweat to Jerzy's chest from a spray bottle. Then the angle was reversed for another few takes. "I'll come back for you, you son of a bitch!" and then—zoom!—down the highway.

"More sweat, Heidi!" Marijan yelled. With Jerzy becoming downright grotesque, the crew took to calling them Dr. Jekyll and Heidi.

The set was reshuffled for Milner's production stills. As Rudy raced head-on towards him, Milner's stance spread and his feet dug deepening trenches in the sand. He snapped away, the electric winder whirring through an entire roll of film before he leaped out of the way to safety. I laughed heartily from my perch behind the reinforced girders of the tower.

Meanwhile Rudy's chesty girlfriend got so drunk on the free beer, a simple smile was enough to shift her center of gravity and send her toppling over into the lap of a happy electrician. At one point beer foamed down the front of her shirt. "Don't worry," counseled Harry, "It's good for the skin."

They continued shooting, and I went out back again. Drained of energy, of enthusiasm, I began nodding in a stiff-backed chair, my head bobbing. I just couldn't stay awake. I'd stare at the sky, trying to guess which quarter would hurl the next bolt of silent lightning, but would invariably sink into a half-sleep again, only to be woken by the roar of Rudy's cycle. I smiled at a dead tarantula in the broken fish tank beside me. "You and me, buddy," I said.

A woman sat in a circle of empty chairs sewing all manner of flora to a hat and veil. She actually looked familiar. During a free moment I asked Martin who she was. An actress? Not that he knew of. Her name was Ute. When I sat with her, I kept racking my memory, trying to place her. She asked where I live.

"New York."
"Me, too."
"Where?"

Two blocks from me, that's where. "Every Saturday night at 11:30 I go to buy the Times on the corner of 86th Street and Second Avenue," she revealed, narrowing it down that much more. It hadn't occurred to me that I might know her from my own experience. I began thinking opportunistically, maybe she can help me get work in film, perhaps if we became friends...

For dull as it all seemed on location, as prolonged as each interminable moment became, and far as filming seemed to be from film, I ached to become a part of it. Even this one. Upon arriving, one fantasy had been meeting the film's director, who'd say, "Perfect—we needed someone like you, and here you are!" Though acting wasn't the goal, screenwriting was. Of course none of this happened. Nor did it occur to me that involvement, here or elsewhere, would take more than simply standing around having it *in mind*.

I looked at her as she sewed. She smiled. I huffed. Yet again I was a bystander. I was still years from leaving a teaching job I'd only accepted for the time being. I wanted to work in film, to live abroad, to travel. I did travel, incessantly, but with no ultimate purpose other than flight. And I wanted to write. I'd even set off on this summer-long train journey as a writing project out of which no publication would ever come. I was stuck, and being there on location only compounded it.

"Well, see you in New York sometime," I said, rising to walk away.

Beside me were railroad tracks that stretched into the distance in unwavering double lines. There, too, the obligatory black and white striped railway gate and dangling red lantern. Though I'd only been off the train a single day, I already began thinking about climbing aboard again. The urge wasn't so much to be elsewhere as to be in the process of going. I hardly cared where I'd end up. I stood in the middle of the tracks on a brittle cross-tie and snapped one of surprisingly few pictures. After strolling down the adjacent dirt road a few hundred yards, I turned, said aloud, "Desert...Texas...film..." then came back.

Soon I had the opportunity for a ride back to the hotel. Victor, a native of El Paso who'd been hired to handle the microphone boom, took the sharp curves of the highway at eighty miles per hour while playing his Hohner harmonica. He squeezed out a broken blues, and, as we approached the lights of the city scattered along the dry mountains, said, "I'd leave here first thing if I could only think of somewhere to go." He pulled up to the Hotel Plaza. I had to tumble out of the window, since the door had jammed shut.

It was 4 AM, and a lone Chicano stood on the corner at the bus stop. I knew as a fact the buses wouldn't run until 7. He was standing by a traffic light that looked redder than any I'd ever seen. From the opposite direction came a disheveled middle-aged hired-hand of a man. The grit on his face looked like a fistful of gravel ground into dried mud. "Hey, man, got a cigarette?" he asked me.

"No, sorry."

So he approached the Chicano. "Hey, hombre, got a cigaretto?" Bi-lingual. I was impressed.

The next morning Martin and I ate an overpriced breakfast served by waiters who brought nothing of what we'd ordered and mounds of what we hadn't. It was the crew's first day off in a week. With *Nothing Left to Lose* T-shirts they headed to the pool. Martin and I stepped out to walk to the Mexican border. Martin is tall, slim, with steel-rimmed glasses and close-cropped blond hair. He seems to withdraw from his own size and speaks so softly it's easy to miss half of what he says. We'd met in New York the year before, introduced by mutual friends, and had corresponded ever since. We wrote, mostly, of what we intended to do, and even discussed writing a film together. So I came to El Paso, where he worked and I watched.

Approaching the border, the fancier commercial shops of the city center degraded into dilapidated storefronts selling used clothes by the pound. Cab drivers shouted aggressively, "Cab to the border. Good time in Mexico, hombre. I show you."

Where El Paso and Ciudad Juarez meet in uneasy proximity, the Rio Grande is a lie. It is shallow, only about twenty feet wide, banked by concrete and split in half by barbed wire. On the El Paso side, Border Patrol vans traversed the streets. Behind their smoked-glass windows sat huddled Mexicans, their heads downcast. They sneak back and forth endlessly, ever in search of a living wage, and have reduced the Border Patrol to an ill-tempered shuttle service.

We headed back toward the train station, and I picked up my bags from the luggage check. There were the cinder blocks I'd tripped over, and beside them stood a stocky man with thick, matted black hair webbed over the top of his bald head. He was puffing away on a rancid-smelling cigar. Though it was well over 110 degrees and there was no shelter from the sun, he wore corduroys and a long-sleeved flannel shirt.

Martin climbed on board to see me off. We stood together a moment, silently, in the midst of a time-honored scene, the railway-station good bye.

"Just think how many films used this one," I said.

"*North by Northwest*," Martin replied, and I scanned the crowd to see who would be my Eva Marie Saint.

But like a film set and so unlike a film, the scene dragged on and the exquisite momentum of boarding, hoisting luggage onto the top racks, and hasty, heart-felt farewells got bogged down in last-minute loading, delayed fueling, and Martin and I rather awkwardly running out of words.

A year later we repeated the scene in Berlin as I was heading off on the night train to Warsaw. "I seem to always be taking you to trains," he said then, "and I stay still." I was surprised, for what I remembered most of my leave-taking in El Paso was a sense of bewilderment, of let-down. And the thoughts: When will my life begin? When will I settle and stop having always to move on again?

Nearly everyone in the train to Los Angeles spoke Spanish. Unlike the rapid-fire of Puerto Rican Spanish in New

York, this was more sensual, leisurely and nuanced. But the Spanish that seemed so welcome upon boarding quickly tried my patience as it became evident that no one had any intention of piping down—not even for a moment. Kids raced up and down the aisle with their parents shouting after them, and to each other.

Sitting next to me, a Chicano man smacked his lips on a juicy peach. He offered the bag, and I reached in to find my fingers sinking into rotting fruit. They were *all* rotten, and decidedly not good for the skin. I withdrew one. "I'll have it after dinner," I said, and threw it out when he wasn't looking. He had a camera moored around his neck and would snap away at scenic views and empty landscapes without discrimination. "I love taking pictures," he enthused. "I photograph *everything*."

He heaved a bulky metal camera case onto his lap—it was more than half empty—and proceeded to show me expensive lenses and the most novel, varied, useless collection of attachments I'd ever seen. There were kaleidoscopic prisms to divide a shot into eight duplicate images, mirrors to aim at a subject without facing him, and a stack of filter cut-outs to frame a picture within improbable outlines. He raced off to photograph a used-car lot.

I smiled to a man across from me who smiled sympathetically back. "You've got a long ride ahead of you," he said, nodding to the empty seat. This man was something of a mystery. My first impression was of someone in his late twenties, but as he talked of years spent here and there—Africa, Central America, Los Angeles, a previous marriage, I gave up guessing and never did ask directly. Though I did get his name, Leon. He was Filipino, and this solved another puzzle. I'd first thought he was Mexican, he'd just been traveling there, but knew this didn't quite fit his eyes, wide features, sparse whiskers and blue Maoist cap. He was born and raised in San Francisco.

I told Leon how I had been passing through vast stretches of the most spectacular scenery, but somehow couldn't get myself to take any pictures. I'd frame a shot, focus, and then put the camera back into its case without pressing the shutter.

– Prima Materia –

"I'm very careful about what images I take in," Leon said.

"Huh?"

"Any image you're exposed to registers in your mind. It becomes a part of you, influences your personality. It changes you. That's why TV is so dangerous—I never watch TV. Photographs, too, if you take too many they clutter up your mind."

The train gathered speed as it rocked back into the desert. I spoke of visiting the film set, and the strangeness of it. How after awhile the set looked real and the desert seemed a construction on a back lot in Hollywood.

"That's what images do to you," he said, pulling at his long, sage-like whiskers. "You didn't see the desert: you saw a movie. Damage has been done."

I nodded, then turned to look out the window. That film set posed questions I wasn't ready to articulate. This was as close as I'd ever gotten to a film, and if anything, I was farther than before from becoming any part of it. I sensed it was my own failing, but didn't really know why. How frustrating it all was, being a perpetual bystander when I should have been working right along with them. As I looked out the window at the sands which were already beginning their slow shift to another terrain, I hungered for involvement.

The cameraman collapsed into his seat. "I just took a whole roll. Beautiful, beautiful," he gushed, shaking his head appreciatively. He reached back into his camera case and grabbed a filter cut-out. "Here, look at this one. This one's my favorite."

I put the view finder to my eyes, and there, framed through a perfect keyhole, I saw the desert reel away from me and vanish beyond the far horizon.

Three Poems

Will Nixon

During the Yankees' August Slump

Fucking Squazzi, he pulled over on Park Avenue & grabbed
his dad's favorite long iron from the trunk
to swing at some cabby's front grill & headlights
for stopping at yellow. So we showed up an hour late for rugby
against Prudential Bache loaded with ex-cons
from the mail room. Already, our side was down two tries
& a concussion with a tornado watch threatening from New Jersey.
My first scrimmage I blacked out under the pileup
of muddy thighs & sharp cleats,
so they dumped ice water on my face
& laid me on the sidelines that smelled like goose shit
until I stopped watching glassine caterpillars
crawling on the sky. Sometimes I hated the financial league.
Then Squazzi yelled Yo Pussy & elbowed some teeth
& the fight started after poor Spike caught a head butt & squirted
his nose like Puttanesca sauce our third game running.
I got one good shot at a knee

& woke up in an EMS truck with my intravenous bag swinging
like ship rigging in a hurricane
the way the driver dodged cross-town traffic & curbs.
Squazzi in the shotgun seat cursed at bicycle messengers,
while the medic pressing my fingernails white
said I was dehydrated from tequila shots last night,
then asked if I could feel the dislocated knuckle of my pinkie
or my bruised ribs & groin. I couldn't answer
from my oxygen mask, but I saw a minnow of blood swim up
my intravenous tube & wished I could wake up
in Connecticut & go sailing like I was supposed to before Squazzi called.

— *Prima Materia* —

Now he was cursing the driver for voting Pedro Martinez
an All Star & the medic was forgetting my pulse
& next thing, I woke up under blue lights buzzing like patio zappers
in the emergency hall beside a mummy face
on a gurney with more tubes up its nose than a distributor cap.
Squazzi got booted for pinching a nurse,
but I couldn't talk anyway with my tongue dried out,
my brain reeling from weird dreams after every two minutes
of sleep. All the doctors did
was order more intravenous until I had to piss like a horse
without leaving my gurney, so the nurse
handed me a bent-necked bottle
that echoed down the hallway while the intercom
announced a chaplain's call on line three.

That night I didn't find Squazzi until 10:30 at Rusty's
in Times Square making a 32,000 point run on topless pinball
after his first blow job upstairs. The bartender
with a fake eye that should've soaked overnight in a Bloody Mary
to match his bloodshot stare
saw my hospital bracelet & said,
You guys've been coming in all night.
They letting you out on some kinda holiday?
I shrugged & grabbed a stool graffitied with love signs.
All I wanted was to catch the Yankees late night
at Seattle over peanuts & gold fish & watered beer.
But Squazzi missed three spares
on the table bowling machine & demanded fresh table wax
by sliding his empty mug down the bar
into a multiple collision with a hooker's Manhattan
& sequin purse. She pulled an ivory knife
while the bartender raised his Louisville Slugger,
so Squazzi & I stepped outside under the golden marquee
of cocktail dancers with cherry nipples
& tried to remember
where he'd parked his father's car.

– Will Nixon –

Bosnia, Catskills

Remember the week military helicopters played hide-and-seek
in our mountains, hopping ridges and raking the forest
with propeller gusts? How fast they vanished?
Training for Bosnia we read afterwards in the papers.

So little did I know about that strife during my first years alone
in my cabin with no radio or health insurance,
my doorway guarded by nothing more than a phoebe's nest,
I decided to hike up for my own war rehearsal.

You ask: Why carry somebody else's misery
along with your day pack of fruit bars and compass,
spare socks and weathered copy of *Turtle Island*?
Isn't your own sadness good enough?

Yes, but please understand how little is needed
to imagine a pileated woodpecker hole as a stray explosion
the size of my face. What about the scattered bones,
the hobblebushes with heart-shaped leaves already turning

the bandage blood of autumn? My cherished solitude
grows sick with silence, as if a sniper is waiting for his best shot.
This moment could be my last: kneeling
for nothing more than to check the freshness
of porcupine scat piled before a wedge in the rocks.

Or this: wondering if any Bosnians heard the same song
after the helicopters left, the red-eyed vireo in the canopy:
Here-I-am. Where-are-you? Here-I-am. Where-are-you? Here-I-am.

You say: Perhaps you have a weakness for death.
We've seen you in our headlights: The one who stops

— *Prima Materia* —

and wears work gloves to drag dead fawns off the road.
Haven't you learned how many are still to come?

Hungry, I choose a mossy log and unwrap a fruit bar
while a chipmunk hunches at the end, fiercely shivering its tail.
I would answer these questions, but the contrail
climbing the blue sky has lost the innocence of clouds.

– *Will Nixon* –

The Howler Monkey's Eyes

My crumpled Kleenex catches yellow tears,
runaway drips from the nurse's dropper
dilating my suspect eyes in the office dusk.
All the light box letters blurred below the tabloid
T O L Z P. I couldn't read
the last week of my tropical vacation
without palming my left eye like a pirate patch
so book print wouldn't wear caterpillar fur.
Had I damaged myself with binoculars,
tracking scarlet macaws too close to the sun?
Had I opened my eyes to parasites
in the warm surf? Had I drawn a mosquito
from the rainforest carrying a virus for blindness,
the local curse of paradise?

Every afternoon, howler monkeys
protested thunderstorms with scraping groans
that must have cost every inch
of their throats. Lying in my hammock,
I struggled through an illustrated history of snakes
bookmarked by my plane ticket home.

In his tailored suit, heather green with heavy cuffs,
the bearded ophthalmologist studies my backlit X-rays
without a wrinkle in his jacket: A formal job,
educating patients about oncoming blindness.
He begins by asking how I'm doing. I've felt better, I admit.
Haven't we all? he says. *And the Mets still can't win a game.*
He cups my chin onto a metal frame that holds my face
for examination. The smell on his fingers
might be Phisohex, my mother's favorite soap.
Her eyes now given to science.

— *Prima Materia* —

Don't blink, he says, donning a fluorescent miner's lamp
that fills my sight with a bluish disk of light
so large the dark edges keep slipping from my peripheral vision.
He studies my eyes as tiny caverns of retina hairs,
sees through the poets' favorite mirrors
of love and mystery. I mean to ask:
Have you looked into a howler monkey's eyes
and seen a million years dissolve?
Have you shared the fear older than words?

He explains: *The eyes are layered like onions*
with protective membranes. Your problem
is a little moisture has leaked onto the dry retina,
a common inconvenience at your age.

On his rolling stool, he dictates my condition
into a pocket tape recorder, finishes
with Period. I thank him for absolving paradise,
pay by credit card, step outside
into a parking lot brutal with sunshine,
every chrome reflection as molten as the sun's core.
Dilated, I see the light that drove the angels from this world.

Just a Riffle

Bob Bachner

We weren't more'n a mile down river, when the little fucker starts loosening the straps on the row of duffel bags I spent ten or fifteen minutes packing in tight just a half-hour ago, at the Lee's Ferry put-in, while Jan was telling them all kinds of useful things like they should keep in their day-packs what they were going to want until we stopped for the night. He pulls loose the strap that runs across the boat through the handles and tugs his loose and, of course, about four bags fall off the pile, but at least they stay inside the boat.

"Sorry, Captain," he says, without even looking at me, and kneels down and starts to put back the bags. The girl's face twitches before she turns to take a particularly serious look at the scenery.

I try to keep the edge off my voice. "Just leave them there, Mr. Gordon, I'll fix them in a minute."

"Call me Lenny, Captain," he says, sounding a little surprised that I was smart enough to read his name printed with a red marker on two-inch adhesive tape on his duffel bag.

"O.K., Lenny, if you'll stop calling me Captain. My name is Jake and we're not in the Navy." This time I left a little edge on it. You let some asshole make enough fun of you, and next thing, nobody pays any attention, which makes it take twice as long to get things done, and, besides, I don't get paid to take crap for five days running.

"Right on, Jake," he says cheerfully. "And this is my daughter Vanessa," and he points to the girl who is now looking down into the river like she would rather be under the water than where she is, but of course she has to turn around to acknowledge the introduction, which she does by turning up the corners of her mouth just enough to tell me that it's not my fault that she's probably going to kill herself before we even make that evening's camp.

She's nice-looking, about sixteen, like my own daughter, but where Jeannie, last time I saw her, was piling on the jewelry and the make-up, this girl wears neither. She has one of those unisex faces, smooth even features, still too much kid in them to tell what she's going to look like. She obviously doesn't want any attention right now, so I turn to the middle-aged couple in the back of the boat. "I didn't get your names, folks."

"We're Hank and Sally Rice," the woman answers, and her husband nods his head just in case I didn't believe her. "We're from Spokane," he says, and she nods her head.

"Run any of the rivers up that way?" I ask, knowing damn well they have, an outdoor couple wearing comfortable long pants faded from wear, and big floppy hats against the sun, and with years of weather on the backs of their hands and in the gullies on their faces. We compare notes on the Salmon, which I ran a few years ago.

Meanwhile, my friend up front has opened his duffel and is pulling on what looks like a pair of black pants.

"Hey, Lenny," I say, and this time I don't even try to sound pleasant, "we're going to hit some white water around the next bend. You better get back to your seat, pronto. And what the hell are you putting on there, anyway?"

"What's the matter, Jake, haven't you ever seen a wet suit before?" and sure enough, he pulls the damn thing up over his shoulders and zips it up tight with a proud grin, like a kid who just learned how to put on his bunny suit himself.

We're getting close to Frenchman's Rapid, just a riffle, really, but you want to be particularly careful when you're first starting off. So, with tying down the bags Lenny messed up and getting everyone back in place and taking a few strokes of the oars to keep the boat steady as we slid and rolled through the waves, I'm pretty busy for a while. We get through just fine, and I look back and see the other boats bouncing along, and one, two, three, four they're out, too.

It's Jan and me and Bill Geary and a kid named Stoney in the passenger boats, and Bill's girlfriend Melinda and another girl named Elaine in the supply boat. Jan and her husband, Buck Niedergang, own the outfit, a dozen boats and equipment stacked in a shed behind their house in Flagstaff all winter, floating down the Colorado four or five in a row, like big yellow ducks, from May through September. Everything's carefully planned, no accidents, no surprises, just the way I like it.

When Lenny starts to go over the side, I keep my mouth shut. It's a calm stretch for the next mile or so, and, as long as he keeps his life jacket on, there's no danger. They don't stay in more than a few minutes, anyway. An ordinary wet suit isn't designed for water temperature in the forties. Maybe freezing his ass will keep him off mine.

That's about how it works, although he's world-class stubborn and stays in about twice as long as I thought he would. I don't hear much out of him for the rest of the afternoon, which improves my disposition. The girl relaxes a bit, too, but still doesn't open her mouth unless someone asks her a direct question.

That night, in camp, Lenny shows he's recovered from his little cool-down. He's kinda small, say five-seven, and wiry. His collarbone sticks out of his T-shirt like the rim of a bowl holding his head. Actually, everything seems to stick out, his nose, his ears, his jaw, his cheekbones, even his eyebrows, but in proportion, so he's not such a bad looking guy. He shows up before dinner, tossing a football up and catching it one-handed, and coaxes his daughter to play catch on the hard sand down by the river.

After a few minutes, Stoney joins them. He's a big blonde kid, a couple of years out of college, where he must have been a jock. He's got the build for it and the kind of self-confidence that comes from scoring touchdowns and knocking in runs.

The girl catches the ball just fine, but throws it side-arm, and Stoney stops to show her the right way, standing next to her, coaching, while her father chases her wild throws. I guess that's not Lenny's idea of fun, because, after almost falling in the river, he fires the ball to Stoney and comes back up to the clumps of twos and threes sitting quietly in the evening cool watching the shadow from the sun behind us claw its way up the red cliff across the river. Suddenly, like he knows someone is watching him, he pulls out a colossal cigar and a fancy knife to trim it and a small flame-thrower to light it and starts puffing away like he's Groucho Marx, firing thick bursts of smoke up into the poor cottonwood he happens to be standing under.

At dinner, the girl sits with Jan and Elaine, so I go over to Bill Geary, who I haven't seen since last summer and immediately get his detailed report on Melinda, who looks pretty much like the girl he had with him last season. I think Bill puts in a standing order up at Berkeley to ship him a new one every spring for a couple'a hundred dollars and last year's girl in trade. He does great with the college crowd, though he never got past the tenth grade himself. I don't know; maybe you're better off without too much education. The degrees haven't done me much good.

I don't get much chance to watch the Gordons, the second day. They're in Jan's boat. I get four high school teachers from Denver. One of them is into geology, which used to be my thing, and we spend most of the day talking about locating oil, which I used to be pretty good at but couldn't do worth shit any more, since everything I haven't forgotten about it has become obsolete.

At the lunch stop, I get the history of the Gordon family from Jan, who is the least nosy person I know, but who somehow seems to attract personal information the way a nice, neat picnic ground attracts litter. Lenny is a lawyer in New York, mostly cases about building construction. Very successful. He and Mrs. Lenny are doing the divorce bit big time. Each is trying to line up Vanessa as an ally at a time of her life when she's not looking to have too much to do with either of them. Vanessa told Jan that she had agreed to go on this trip because Lenny always wanted to but never had because her mother wouldn't go and he shouldn't have to be by himself, and, no offense, she wishes she were on the bike trip with her friend Stacy instead.

Well, that story changes things. A man going through a divorce ought to piss-off a few people, maybe even get into a fight or two, anything to let loose some of the craziness, keep him from sucking it deep inside him where he can't ever get rid of it. I feel a little guilty about getting worked up over a lousy wet suit. So, that evening, after dinner, when he pulls out his cigar, and his daughter, who's been eating with him, gets up and makes a big thing of waving her arms to fan away the smoke and holding her nose and gives him the classic Oh Daddy You're Impossible turn, the one with a big shake of the head and a little shake of the ass, and walks away to join Stoney and Melinda, who are fooling around with a guitar, I stroll over, ease myself down and pull a pint of Jack Daniels out of my windbreaker.

"How about a belt, Lenny?" I ask.

"No thanks, Jake," he answers and his eyebrows drop just a fraction as he looks at me. "How about a cigar?" and he pulls out another black torpedo.

I decline and take a slug of Jack. "I'm sorry to hear you're having trouble in the matrimonial department," I say sympathetically. "I've been through it myself," and I get busy lighting a cigarette, so it doesn't look like I'm watching for a reaction. He doesn't answer, and when I do look back at him I don't see anything in his face except that little bitty frown, so I continue. "It's not much fun while it's going on, but once things get settled, you get over it a lot quicker'n you might think now."

Jake's wisdom: I probably got it off one of those redwood plaques that hang behind bars all over the West.

Lenny pulls on the cigar, lets loose a cloud of insect-killer and asks "So, what happened to you, Jake?"

Sometimes hearing another man's troubles can make yours seem a little easier to handle. So I tell him the Readers Digest version of mine. In the pauses, I can hear Stoney softly singing "Careless Love" and then "Good Night Irene" with the girls coming in on the choruses. When I finish, Lenny stubs out the cigar and says "Thanks Jake, you just reminded me of something very important."

"Patience, Lenny, that's what it takes," I say, feeling pretty good with myself.

"No, Jake, it's that other people's troubles make dull conversation. I think I'll go to bed before I start boring you with mine."

He gets up and goes over to the girl, says something, and, when she shakes her head, stalks away to where the sleeping bags are laid out. So, all I get for trying to be nice to the guy is a put-down. Besides which I start thinking about the look on Carol's face when I told her I was splitting, and I end up killing the pint, neither of which is a good idea.

The third day is only a half-day on the river; I draw an airline pilot, a retired doctor and their wives, all nice, quiet people, more interested in the towering cliffs we're floating through in long, slow bends, than they are in making conversation, which is fine by me. We make camp on a big, comfortable beach. After lunch, Jan and Stoney take the passengers with energy on a hike up a side ravine to where a waterfall makes a little pool, not big enough for real swimming, but it's fun splashing around after an hour's climb in a hundred-ten degrees of heat. I tell Melinda she shouldn't miss it, so she drags Bill along and I get to stay back in camp at the price of a half-hour cleaning up with Elaine. I settle in the shade with a cold beer, which I fetch from a net bag tied to my boat. It's a real nice afternoon and I knock off a letter to Jeannie, about fifty pages of a paperback and three beers before the troops come sweating in, Lenny bouncing along up front with Jan so everyone can see what great shape he's in, and the rest strung out on the path with Vanessa in the back laughing at some joke of Stoney's. It's good to see the kid loosening up and having some fun, even if there's nobody her age around.

It's the birthday of one of the teachers, so dinner becomes a party with a cake and a couple of gag presents and, after dinner, we pass around some wine in paper cups and drink toasts to the poor guy. Then Stoney gets out the guitar and we sing "Happy Birthday" and a bunch of other group songs until it starts getting dark. Three or four people leave and he does a couple of solos, old familiar folk songs, mostly, simple strums on the guitar, nothing that'll get him a recording contract, but pleasant. Then he and Vanessa sing a couple of duets. A shiny, round moon pokes up through a break in the cliff across the river like a new quarter coming out of a coin machine instead of going into it. Jan whispers to me that if she could videotape the scene she could sell out every trip. Everyone's having a good time. Except maybe Lenny, who's sitting a few yards apart from the group, staring into his little paper cup.

— *Prima Materia* —

The next day completes the rotation of the passengers among the four boats. I finally get my turn for the German invasion, two couples from Stuttgart spending four months touring America. We stop for lunch at one of the world's prettiest places, where the Little Colorado joins the big river. It carries particles of clay, in suspension, which coat the rocks so they look like gray, carob-covered nuts. The water is warm, and we row upstream a bit to some mild rapids where you can get some safe kicks shooting down in your life jacket.

Stoney's boat pulls in next to mine. He's got the Gordons today, with the doctor and his wife. Vanessa jumps out to show me the beginnings of blisters she got when Stoney taught her how to row, then runs over to help Melinda and Elaine unload the supply boat for lunch. It's clearly not the same girl I had the first day. Nor is Lenny the same guy. His sulk has turned into a glower. No football today. He gets out of the boat and marches away, without a word to anybody, and plops down in the shade. When lunch is ready, he comes back only long enough to grab a sandwich and a soda and returns to his spot away from everyone else.

After we feed the passengers, I take my beer and sandwich over and sit next to Stoney. "So, how's it going, dude? What happened to get Mr. Sunshine so pissed?" Stoney grins. "Just the old story, Jake. Poppa doesn't like his little girl making eyes at a guy."

"So that's what's going on. You so hard up for women, now, you're after high school kids? You're kinda ugly but not that bad," I say very seriously.

His grin gets bigger. "What can I do, Jake? Melinda's hung up on Bill and Elaine doesn't go for guys. That leaves Vanessa and Jan, and I can't very well screw the boss, can I?" The thought of that almost makes me choke on a mouthful of beer. I tell him to keep it in his pants and stay out of trouble, and he laughs and promises to be good, and we pack up and float back to the river and down to camp. This is the last night for most of the passengers; they'll get off-river at Phantom Ranch the next day, and hike or take mules up to the South Rim and a new batch will come down the trail in the morning to float the longer section of the river to Lake Mead.

When we get into camp, Lenny scurries over to Jan to borrow her fishing rod and takes it over to the girl who is standing with a group going to see some Indian ruins. The group starts walking, and Stoney, at its head, calls out, "Move it baby, the bus is leaving."

The girl gives Lenny a quick peck on the cheek and takes off. He opens his mouth to say something, but it's too late. I duck my head just before he looks around to see if anyone noticed and strolls down to the river for his fishing.

The group starts trickling back in about an hour, Stoney and Vanessa last, about five minutes behind everyone else, just about when Lenny comes over to the fire to dump two trout and the rod in front of Jan. He's got a nasty look on his face, so I casually stroll towards where he is now headed to meet the two, but he ignores Stoney and says something quietly to the kid and they go off to wash up.

"What the fuck are you up to?" I ask Stoney.

"Come on, Jake," he laughs. "Do you think we were making it on the trail? Lighten up a little." He swaggers away. Macho wise-ass.

I keep my eye peeled at dinner, but everything seems cool; the only thing different is that Lenny sticks pretty close to the girl and passes up his after-dinner cigar. Since it's the last night, most of the passengers stick around for a while after dinner. Stoney gets his guitar and there's more singing and another couple of bottles of wine. It starts getting dark, people head for their sleeping bags, and it's just Stoney, Vanessa and Lenny sitting together. I putter around the boxes of gear, check the lines on the boats and generally cruise around, watching to make sure something doesn't explode. Stoney has put down his guitar and he and Lenny are having a big palaver, but I can't catch what they're saying. The kid seems sort of left out; she's sitting with her legs drawn up to her chest, her arms around her knees and her head balanced with the point of her chin on one kneecap, swiveling back and forth so she can look at each of the two men as they talk in turn.

Finally, curiosity gets to be too much and I come sit next to Vanessa. Lenny's asking Stoney about college, like it's for her benefit since she'll be going in a couple of years, but most of the questions are about Stoney's personal experiences. Every time Stoney answers a question, Lenny nods or makes a little comment of approval, sometimes turning to Vanessa or me for back-up, so we, too, can let Stoney know how terrific he is for having made this team or gotten into that fraternity. Then, right away, before anyone can break the flow, the next question comes, always in the same quiet, serious tone, so Stoney can feel comfortable, a little flattered even, that this man is so interested in the details of his life.

Lenny then shifts to questions about courses, and studying and exams. Stoney's no dummy and he did well enough to graduate, but I guess he wasn't a great student, so there's quite a come-down from his athletic accomplishments, but you could never tell it from Lenny's voice. Vanessa shifts position a couple of times and looks at her watch, like maybe she was hoping for some time alone with Stoney, which it doesn't look like she's going to get.

Somehow they've gotten on to girls which gets Vanessa to stop fidgeting. Me, I'm not saying anything. Let Stoney take care of himself. The questions start very general and easy and Stoney relaxes again, but it doesn't take long before they get personal. He looks over at Vanessa once or twice, in embarrassment, before answering, but after all it's her father who's asking the questions, so it must be all right to answer. As it goes on, he starts to stumble once in a while and tries to change the subject, starts to ask Lenny questions, anything to get off the witness stand, but Lenny handles smoothly everything Stoney throws at him and turns it into another question, another polite, simple question.

They've been at it for almost an hour, and now Lenny goes into the present. What is Stoney doing now? Guiding river trips. And in the winter? Ski patrol. Having fun? Sure. Saving any money? No. What about a career? Something will turn up. Like to get high? Booze, mostly. Having fun? Sure. How's the family? Don't see them. Marriage? Ties you down, but maybe some day. What about kids? Other people's are fine. What would you like to accomplish in life? Haven't thought about it much. Having fun? Sure, why do you keep asking me that?

Lenny gets up slowly and stretches, and I wait for the killer answer that will finish the job. Stoney, too, leans forward, for, after that answer, he will explain things, give the right tap to the child's puzzle picture that will cause all the little pieces to fall back into their holes to form that handsome, all-American face instead of the vapid image his own words have made. But, Lenny says nothing, just reaches out his hand to Vanessa who rises and silently goes with him.

It's my good fortune to have them back in my boat the last morning, together with the Rices. It's a lot like the first day; Lenny is cocky and obnoxious, and the girl is down in the dumps. We're going through the black, gnarled rocks of the inner gorge now, where you can't even see the rim. After an hour, we come to Double Header, our last stretch of white water. There's a real tough rapid, followed by about three hundred yards of clear water and then a pretty easy rapid.

Jan goes through first, then the supply boat, then Bill, Stoney, and me. We're doing just fine until a wave sends a few buckets full of water into the Gordons' faces, like has happened a dozen times before, but this one knocks off the kid's sunglasses, and she lets go the rope to grab for them, and the next wave tilts the boat, and she goes sprawling toward the edge, and Lenny lunges for her, and the edge of the boat goes under the next wave, which flips the whole boat over like it was nothing.

I come up in a few seconds. Another wave goes over me, then the life jacket pops me back up and I'm out in clear water. Vanessa is floundering a few feet away and I get there in a couple of strokes and grab her jacket and tell her to keep still, we're not far from the shore and she relaxes. The Rices are on the other side of the river, holding onto the upside-down boat, which is fine. Lenny is floating in the middle of the river. The first two boats are in the second rapid, already, and Bill is too close to stop, but Stoney has seen what happened and is pulling like mad on the oars against the current. But the sonuvabitch, instead of holding position until Lenny floats down to him, is heading crosscurrent towards me.

"Get him, not us!" I scream at Stoney, but he doesn't hear me. I'm swimming as hard as I can to pull the girl over to the bank. I yell again, but Stoney keeps coming our way. It's too late, anyway; Lenny's getting close to the second rapid, but at least he's moving his arms now, and just before he gets to it he leans back and goes in feet first like we tell them to.

I get the kid into the eddy as Stoney arrives, then it's easy getting to shore, and a couple of the Germans jump out and help us up. She looks for her father and gets hysterical when I tell her what happened, and she starts scrambling along the bank headed downstream, the Germans and me after her, and she comes a lot closer to killing herself on the rocks than she did in the water. When we get about midway in the second rapid we can see where all the boats are, further down, pulled over to the shore and Lenny, climbing out of one of them and starting to stumble back up towards us, and then he sees us coming and sits down. We get there in a few minutes and the two of them are crying all over each other, and she's fine and the doctor says all Lenny's got is a few bruises, and Mrs. Rice says it was kind of fun, climbing onto the upside-down boat and going through that way, and we put everything together and limp on into Phantom Ranch, and that's the last I see of Mr. Leonard Gordon. And I don't think I'm going to look him up if I get to New York, either.

What with everything, we're pretty late pulling out of Phantom Ranch with the new passengers and getting to that night's campsite, and it's some time before I get a chance to talk to Stoney alone. I have to follow him down the path to the crapper.

"Wait up, kid," I say, "I want to talk to you." So he stops. "What the fuck were you doing back there on the river? Why didn't you pick up Lenny? Even if you didn't hear me yell, you could see I had the girl."

His handsome face looks a little puzzled. "Come on, Jake, why are you making such a big thing of it? He had his jacket on, and you know as well as I do that the second part of Double Header is nothing, just a riffle. It makes a good name, that's all."

"Stoney, the man could have drowned or cracked his skull open. You'd have that happen to someone just because he made you look like an asshole in front of a girl?"

"I don't know what you're talking about. Besides, who dumped him in the river in the first place? Let's have a slug of Jack and forget it."

I don't know whether it's the tone of his voice or the look on his face, but I get real pissed-off and take a swing at him which misses and I find myself on my ass with a terrible pain in the side of my face which turns out to be a broken jaw. Stoney couldn't be more sorry and half carries me the next morning up the little trail that backtracks to Phantom Ranch where they pack me on a mule that takes me to the South Rim where I end up in the hospital.

That's about the end of the story, except I have to stay off the river while the jaw is healing so I drive to Houston to say hello to Jeannie. Carol is nice enough to invite me for dinner, which in my case, is mostly mashed potatoes. I tell them the story of how I got myself all wired up, and they both shake their heads and tell me they always knew I was an idiot. I had hoped for some time alone with Jeannie, but of course some punk comes after her halfway through the meal, so Carol and I finish by ourselves. It feels good though, to be sitting with her over coffee, quietly talking about our daughter, like nothing ever happened. After a while, Carol gets up to clear the table, turns down my offer to help with the dishes, and leads me to the front door. She's looking terrific and I'm feeling like a kid leaving a girl off after their first date. I kind of reach out for her, but she fends me off easily and asks, "So, Jake, why did you swing at Stoney, anyway?" I just shrug my shoulders as I turn to head back to the motel for three days of booze and TV before going back to Flagstaff. I mean, who the fuck knows why they do anything?

Love | Crime | Truth | Lies

Learning to Jump

Minda Zetlin

This is a story about love, but I am going to start with horses. Three years ago, I broke my arm while trying to ride my first cross-country jump course. I heard the bone break—loud as a gunshot, or so it seemed—when I hit the ground. Afterward, I knew it was broken for sure when I felt the pieces moving inside my arm.

I handled it well whenever anyone was looking. I pinned the number I'd been wearing for the jumping competition to the sling, to show I hadn't broken my sense of humor. Then I phoned the Gentleman (an exceedingly well dressed man who shared my apartment and bed for five years) from the hospital waiting room. I warned him that when I came home for dinner, I'd be wearing an impressive fiberglass cast.

When no one could see, I fell apart. I cried alone in the x-ray lab, waiting to find out what the x-ray would say when I knew perfectly well what it would say. It wasn't so much because it hurt; what drove me crazy was knowing I'd screwed up. I kept scolding myself: You idiot! If only you'd committed yourself to the jump, kept your weight back, and your legs steady on the horse, he would have jumped it instead of swerving away! And when he swerved, if you'd been determined, I bet you could have stayed on. And if you did have to fall off, why on earth did you have to stick out your arm like that? If only you'd been a little more forceful, a little more careful, used a little more common sense, this never would have happened.

Then there was the helplessness. Something about needing other people to do things for me infuriated me beyond endurance. For months, friendly strangers would offer to help me on with my coat, and if I didn't catch myself in time, I would snap at them to stay away. The Gentleman had a penchant for making roasts and steaks for Sunday dinner, which I normally loved. But during that broken arm, instead of feeling gratitude at having a live-in lover who cooked for me, I would sit there glowering while he cut up my meat.

It turned out to be an awful break, which took forever to heal. It was more than five months until the doctor said I could ride again, but as soon as he did, I got back on. To my surprise, I was no more afraid of riding after the accident than I had been before. But then, that had always been my problem. Fear, when you're on a horse, is the most dangerous thing in the world. It can make your body stiff. In my case, it makes me pull my weight forward at exactly those moments when it would be safer to keep it back. It can make you wishy-washy in your signals, and that almost always leads to trouble. The fact that I was literally scared stiff that day probably is why I broke my arm in the first place.

Why did I go back, if I was so scared? For one thing, I hate giving in to fear. Edith hates it. Edith is my name for that voice—is there anyone who doesn't have one?—that passes continual judgment on everything I do. "You can't give in to fear," Edith said. "Live your life that way, and you'll come to no good. Now get back on that horse!"

So I did. And it turned out that for all the aches and pains and bruises, and the frustration at doing something I'm not naturally good at, riding makes me very happy. So you see, it was only partly Edith. It was also love.

So OK. His name was Tom. Well, actually it wasn't, but it might as well have been: Tom was the name of one of two boys I was torturously, hopelessly in love with in high school, and he had the same name as the other.

He was very, very bald. "Cue-ball bald," I said to my friend Sam, having learned long ago how much safer it is to laugh at the things that matter to me most. Tom was a little self-conscious about his baldness, but, all things considered, remarkably little. He kept the little hair he had left cut very short, even shaved it altogether for a period before he met me, so he said. Another time, for some other reason, he showed me a picture of himself from seven years earlier.

"Do you think I had much more hair then?" he asked.

I peered at the picture, then at his current head. "No, not much."

"Good, maybe it's finally slowed."

Sure, the way a forest fire slows when there's nothing left but a few charred trunks. "Um, I don't think people get much balder than you," I said.

It was what I meant, and I'm a person who prides herself on saying what she means, especially to men, but even for me, that was awfully blunt.

"I mean..." I tried to salvage, "I had an uncle who was very bald once, he went bald early like you and, well, he's dead now, but when I first met him he was in his sixties and he had only slightly less hair than you do now..."

He laughed good-naturedly. "Go ahead," he said, "squirm some more."

I loved him for that, him and his bald head. Go ahead, squirm some more. That was the kind of thing I fell for.

I should tell you right now, before it's too late, that I don't have a friend Sam. I have lots of friends. OK, maybe not lots, but enough, and they've all, at one time or another, listened to me and talked to me about my love life, just as I've listened and talked about their love lives, and rather than stop and introduce a new one every time I come to one, I figured I'd call them all Sam. I think you know what I mean, because everyone, it seems to me, has had a Sam and been a Sam at one time or another. Some of my Sams are girls, some are boys, and I keep hoping that someday that will help me get some perspective on this business of men and women.

Here's another thing I fell for: his answering machine

message. I'll admit, that may sound odd, but if you think about it, answering machine messages are the most essential form of self-expression we have in our modern world. On his, he plays the bass. That's what he does, more or less, play the bass, and I can't even be bothered to turn it into something else because I can't think of another instrument that's so...well, basic: melodic and rhythmic and sensual and very, very sexy.

"It's a sound that drops right down into you." I've said that to him in my imagination a thousand times, lightly drawing a line with one finger from my hairline down to my belly button to illustrate. It's a sound that seems to suck up out of the earth itself.

So there he is, playing the bass in a band, a little snatch of a song, people shouting with plain musical joy in the background the way people do at the beginning of certain songs. "It's Tom," he says. "I'm not here right now. Um, talk for a while." Pause. "Have fun..."

Have fun. For ages, I heard that answering-machine tune in my mind wherever I went, and even now I can bring it back easily. Have fun. I fell in love with that, and him.

We met...oh, I could make up how we met. It would be fun, too, meetings in New York City are always a blast to write. We got stuck in a subway car for three hours with the lights out, and the only other people there were either winos or religious fanatics. I helped him and several of his buddies lift and move a car that had double-parked in front of his. There are countless fun ways two people can meet in fiction in New York City. In fact, I find it damned difficult, so the truth is, we met through a personal ad (mine, not his). I'm ashamed about it and embarrassed as hell, which is why, Edith says, I had better own up and tell you.

We talked on the phone several times first. We were both cautious and busy, the way people are in New York, even when they're lonely at the same time. "Tom" became this disembodied voice I talked to, late at night, with a cat curled up on my lap. Even after I met him, the Tom of the late-night phone conversations remained a separate entity in my mind, so that I would be surprised to learn that the Tom in front of me remembered those conversations.

The day that we were finally supposed to meet, I forgot our appointment. Or rather, I remembered it wrong: I thought we had tentative plans to meet for lunch, and he was supposed to call and confirm the night before; in fact, we had definite plans, and I was supposed to call him at noon and decide where. I noted that he didn't call the previous evening, then put him out of my mind so completely that when the phone rang at 12:30 the next day, I was sitting there with greasy hair, eating a slice of pizza and planning a long, luxurious bath afterward.

"This is Tom. Are we having lunch?"

Like magic, the corrected memory of our arrangement came flooding back, now that it was one minute too late to act on it. There was no choice but to admit that I had screwed up. Edith was having a field day.

Wincing with embarrassment, I put the pizza in the refrigerator and promised to meet him in an hour. He would know me, I added, by my slightly damp hair.

Still, there was something very good about the fact that I'd forgotten him, and it was this: I had proven how eager I wasn't. Granted, by doing a stupid thing, but nevertheless, I'd demonstrated that I didn't have my whole life riding on this encounter, that I wasn't harboring premature fantasies of marriage, or any other crazy idea you might attribute to the purveyor of a personal ad. In my mind, at least, I was now free to be myself. He wasn't going to think I was throwing myself at him when I had already done something neglectful.

I thought about this as I washed my hair and dressed: black pants and a black-and-white cotton top I loved, with a wide neck that dipped off the shoulder, exposing the straps of a turquoise bra I was wearing underneath. Bright red lipstick, of course, and for earrings, a dark tangle of green wires that I'd bought from a woman I'd found making them in a doorway in

Soho. It was what you'd call the real me, as really me as my clothes get, and I never would have dressed that way if I hadn't first shown my disdain by forgetting our appointment.

Outside the restaurant, a few doors away, I ran into someone I knew and stood talking to him for a few seconds, partly because I wanted to talk to him, partly because I thought that if Tom came along while I was doing it, it would further help to prove I wasn't dying of loneliness. He did come along, or rather he walked over from the door of the restaurant, where he'd stationed himself to wait for me. He had recognized me instantly, though I don't know whether it was because my hair still was damp, or because his musician's ear couldn't mistake my voice.

What did I think of him at that moment? Somehow it seems very important to remember. Pixie-like, I think, is what I would have said. I mean, there was that bald head, and the goatee and, though I didn't see it right away, a mischievous twinkle in his eyes. He had described himself as "balding," which, you may have gathered, was a bit of an understatement. ("He's done balded," I told Sam later), but I didn't mind. Instead of hair, he had freckles on his scalp, which conjured images for me of a healthy life lived out in the sun.

I didn't think he was strikingly handsome, but OK. Not bad looking. He didn't look as muscle-bound as I'd expected, since he'd told me how much time he spent working out, but, I would eventually learn, he was very strong indeed. Strong enough to lift me down from the windowsill when I'd been putting plants outside to get some sun, strong enough to carry me from wherever we happened to be to the bed, just like they always do in the movies.

It seems odd to remember it now, that there was ever a time I could stand and look at him without thinking much of anything. Without reacting.

There's an interesting thing about the personals: you can't pretend. You know what I mean. You know the way we do, in New York City: Oh I'm so popular, oh I'm so busy, oh I can barely get all my work done, oh I don't really have time for anyone in my life right now.

Forget it. Who are you kidding? You have the time, and you have the need, or you wouldn't be there at all, and everyone knows it. And so, when we finally sat down to have lunch together, that was there, sitting on the table between the sushi and the pickled ginger: So, whaddaya think? Are you right for me? Am I right for you? Whaddaya say we try and find out? I suppose it's one reason why things got so...out of hand so very quickly.

That first date was a marathon conversation. He was amazed to be thirty-four, and playing in a band whose other members were still undergraduates. "We're taking a couple of weeks off so they can study for their midterms," he said. "What's next, taking time out for bar mitzvahs?"

I was simply amazed to be thirty at all. We talked about my work and his past. We talked about Twin Peaks, and why I seemed to be the only young intellectual in New York who didn't watch it. We talked about his having been a lawyer and why he hadn't liked it ("My guy says this and your guy says the opposite, and the truth is probably somewhere in the middle," he would say to opposing counsel, trying to take a shortcut to a settlement. "Oh, so you admit your client is lying," would inevitably be the reply.)

Tom tried ever so gently to find out exactly why I'd forgotten our appointment—that is to say, the underlying psychological reason. It was another thing that made me like him immensely. I realize, of course, that this isn't the sort of quality most people would find endearing, but then most people hadn't spent five years with the Gentleman, a man who would never admit there was an underlying reason for anything. But here was Tom, unwilling to take things at face value, ready to look below the surface and risk finding whatever he might find. It was another thing I fell in love with.

We kept on talking until the restaurant closed for the afternoon and, in a polite, Japanese way, threw us out. Then we split a dish of chocolate-and-hazelnut ice cream at an Italian cafe and talked some more, and then he walked me home.

I didn't invite him in, of course. I mean, I liked him and everything, but I had just met him and he was, after all, a personal ad respondent. So instead, we leaned on the mailbox outside my building, talking for another half hour or so, while I nodded to my various neighbors on their way in and out.

Meanwhile, I finished sizing him up. He seemed not too bad. Worth a second look, certainly, though it still seems odd to me now that this was all I felt then. There was a band I loved playing at a benefit the following night, an Afro-Reggae-Pop band from upstate that no one I'd ever met in the city until him had even heard of. But because he knew everything there was to know about rock music, or so it seemed to me, he knew not only who they were but that they would be playing at this benefit, and he invited me. And I agreed to go.

The last thing I did before I went inside was point out my apartment. It wasn't hard to spot: mine was the only window on the whole front of the building with a window box. It was brimming over with bright pink moss roses, orange marigolds, tiny yellow daisies and deep red mums. Then I had a row of taller, more useful plants crowded between the window box and the window: catnip, basil and late tomatoes. It looked utterly lush, as if someone had uprooted two square feet of the Amazon Jungle, and transplanted them to my second-story ledge. Watching him looking up at it, I realized it was almost too revealing.

Have you been wondering why I started with horses? I certainly meant to get back to them before this. There was a reason: I had decided that jumping is very much like life. I'm not very good at jumping, and so I spend a lot of time thinking about it. Or maybe it's the other way around: the reason I'm not very good is that I think about it so much. In jumping, as in life, too much thinking and being afraid are the things that screw me up the most.

"Throw your heart over the jump and your horse will follow." I read that in Isak Dinesen somewhere, and was very taken with it. And so, when I started learning to jump, that's what I would try to do. I actually wound up bobbing my shoulders unconsciously—as if I were literally trying to fling my heart out through my rib cage and over the crossbars—a movement which mystified my riding teachers.

Later, I read a biography of Isak Dinesen and found out that she really hadn't been a very good horsewoman after all. The epigraph of *Out of Africa* is "Equitare, Arcum tendere, Veritatem dicere," which is from Nietzsche and means "To ride, To shoot with a bow, To tell the truth." It turns out, or so said her brother, that she couldn't ride, and was a lousy shot, and that throughout *Out of Africa*, supposedly a memoir, she blithely rearranged the truth whenever it suited her.

But I don't even care. She was right: if you're going to go at a jump, then you can't hold back. Hold back, and you'll get a refusal, or a clumsy little jump called a "stop-and-pop" that's much more likely to unseat you. If you really want to take a jump, then you have to commit, give up the possibility of changing your mind at the last second, trust the horse, and most of all your own balance. And of course, if despite your best efforts your horse manages a stock-still refusal at the last moment, you yourself will probably go sailing on over the jump anyway.

We didn't go to the benefit, after all. It was my fault: I'd tried to pack too many appointments into that evening, and couldn't meet him till late, which is usually fine for dancing, but turned out not to be fine for this particular event. Instead, we met at a neat little place on Houston Street: it has oddly shaped tables and a ceiling that appears to be made entirely of sweaters, and if you know where I'm talking about, then you're very hip indeed, and if you don't you should go try to find out because

1) it's worth knowing about and 2) you'll probably find a lot of other interesting places along the way.

Anyway, I got there right before midnight, and he was waiting for me near the door. I was wearing blue pants, a patterned green Soho-type T-shirt with the neck cut out, brightly colored wooden African beads and long blue glass earrings that sparkled in the light. He gazed.

We drank beer for a long time, sitting away from the crowd, in the glow of the neon by the picture window and talked some more. Eventually, he asked if I wanted to go listen to the music in the other room, although, he said, he'd be perfectly happy to keep on talking.

"Let's go," I said. "We're getting along well and all, but eventually we will run out of things to talk about."

I think back on this, and Edith snorts: Boy, was I wrong! First of all, we never would run out of things to talk about. And second of all, it wouldn't be long until I'd start yearning, aching almost, for the chance to just sit and talk. Not that he didn't want to talk, he was almost as garrulous as I was, it's just that there were so many other things going on. So much fire, so much hunger. Too much to calmly tell each other the stories of our lives.

The music was interesting, and, at times, quite odd. I liked some of it, tried to like the rest. He liked it very much, and very obviously, clapped hard, pounded the table and at one point gave a one-man standing ovation. Edith and I had a debate over that one: she was furious at him for embarrassing us that way; I was embarrassed but also charmed—he seemed so unselfconscious.

Afterward, we snuck into the benefit. By that time, it was very late, after 3:00, and the ticket takers had long since stopped guarding the doors, so there was no one to object. A salsa band was playing.

"You'll have to teach me how to dance to this music," Tom said, for I had told him that the Gentleman and I had been ballroom dancers together, and that I liked salsa because it reminded me of mambo.

"Oh, just dance!" I said, and I bet he liked that. But watching me dance, I think, is when it really happened for him. Because that's one thing, in my whole over-examined life, that I do well, without too much thinking and without holding back. I have the thorough understanding of rhythm that comes from many hours spent listening to African music, and a pretty good idea of how to move to it. And years of observation have convinced me that the only way it's possible to look foolish while dancing is by doing it half-heartedly.

By the time he walked me home, it was after 4:00, late even for a couple of night owls like us. Outside my door, he stood and kissed me. He had a method for this: first he would sort of straddle his legs apart, which made up for some of the eight-inch difference in our heights. Then he would kiss me, long, slow and thoughtful, his tongue exploring the inside of my mouth. Then he would sigh, as if all were right with the world.

He asked me out for the following Monday, which was two days away. "Three dates in four days?" Edith exclaimed. "Is he out of his mind? Don't even think about it."

"I don't know," I told him. "I have to think about it." Then I thought about it, and said yes.

We went out dancing again, once again it was very late, and we were standing in the doorway of my building, exchanging kisses that were punctuated from time to time with his sighs.

"What's the sighing about?" I finally asked.

He squared his shoulders, told me he loved kissing me, and asked forthrightly if he might spend the night.

Edith, for once, had no opinion on this subject. She's a plethora of shouldn'ts and shoulds, but, like me, she was raised during the sexual revolution, and if anything, she thinks I'm not adventurous enough. She worries I might be missing some great sexual experiences.

So when I told Tom no, it was really me saying no. Not that I thought I shouldn't, I just wasn't comfortable with the thought of letting him—or anyone—that far into my life. It had been almost exactly a year since the Gentleman left. Now it gave me the willies to think of a new man undressing me, touching my naked body, watching my face contort with pleasure. Especially one I'd only known for four days. On the other hand, I didn't really want to watch him walk away. Mostly, I wanted to talk to him some more. We had so much, I thought by then, we needed to find out about each other. And so, on that understanding, I asked him in.

I know what you're thinking: Yeah, right. Sure, he was going to come in and not expect to get laid. How could you think he meant it? And, alone in your apartment, especially strong as he was, what was to keep him from doing whatever he wanted?

Well, I was sure. I hadn't known him long, but I already knew for a certainty that in this respect, I could trust him. And I was right. We sat on the sofa drinking more beer, talking, sometimes necking, talking some more, while the resistance in me slowly wore away. So that, around 2:00 or so, our arms wrapped around each other, when he said, "Well, if I'm going, I'd better go," I answered, "Well...all right, stay."

I felt a tremor go right through his body when I said that. It was as if I had performed magic.

When exactly did it happen to me? I should be able to remember it in slow motion, like that moment in the movie *Niagara* when the man who's murdered Marilyn heads his boat into the falls, and it teeters on the edge for what seems like forever before plunging over.

Maybe it was after he told me how long it had been since he'd been involved with another woman. He said he found it difficult. Difficult? You? Tom, of the three dates in four days? The one who charmed me with the most direct and

— Prima Materia —

unflinching proposition I've ever gotten from one of your gender?

Because it's you, he answered, everything's different with you—and I felt myself unfurl like a flower.

So we made love, and then we slept, curled up, his arms around me all night long. He didn't even seem to mind my two cats, who, during my year of singlehood, had come to believe they had inalienable rights to the bed.

In the morning, we showered together. He didn't drink coffee and had no time for tea, but while I was in the kitchen getting my own coffee, he snuck up and put his arms around me from behind. It startled me badly, but at the same time, I kind of liked it.

"It's going to be really hard to leave you," he said at last, kissing me over and over, late already when he finally made it out the door.

After he was gone, I found myself leaning against the wall, breathless, a lost cause already. "You can't," I was saying out loud, "you can't, you can't, you can't do this to me."

I felt like such an idiot. You know how it goes, in the cheap paperbacks and bad movie scripts. At some point or another, the character who's falling in love will say: "I don't know what's come over me! I can't eat, I can't sleep, I can't work! All I can do is think about (fill in the blank). Whenever I close my eyes, I see her/his face."

And you think: Give me a break! That old, tired cliche? You're right, of course. But the problem is: how do I write about it now? I've been in love lots of times, but that was the first time I've ever felt so...unhinged. Out of control. It wasn't a pleasant feeling.

But it was an enormous relief. It had been so long since I'd loved anyone but the Gentleman, and splitting up with him had left a lot of scar tissue. I've always said that he and I had all the disadvantages of a marriage but none of the advantages, and one of marriage's biggest disadvantages is that it has only two possible endings: death or divorce. Either one needs to be followed by a period of mourning, but I tried to skip that part. I pretended I wasn't hurting, or not much: a touch of the flu, not walking pneumonia. In a way, I think that made it worse: it's hard to heal a wound you won't admit you have in the first place. "I keep thinking I'm completely over him," I told Sam, "only to discover I've just reached a new stage of getting over him. Maybe married couples—and even de facto married couples—never really do get over each other."

So there I was, world-weary, heartsore and now no longer in my twenties. I felt sure I'd never make a fool of myself over any man again: I thought I just didn't have it in me. Tom showed me I was wrong, and I was very grateful.

Two days after we woke up together, I left on a prearranged visit to my mother's place in the country. "I hope you don't mind listening to me blather on about him for three days," I said in her car, on the way home from the station. (What could she say? "Yes I do! Get back on the train!")

For most of the visit, I lay on my stomach on the guest bed, my feet in the air as if I were in goddamned junior high, writing about him in my journal: "So...my brain's been invaded, it seems."

At four in the morning, when the rest of the household was sleeping and I couldn't, I lay on my back in the dark, listening to tapes of Police albums loud over my Walkman, with the bass turned way up. When I finally fell asleep, I dreamed about him. You may find this hard to believe, but I did, two dreams. In the first, he was helping me feed my cats, clean up my bathroom and get rid of a quantity of large white flying insects that had settled there. I dream about bugs often, they seem to stand for bad feelings of one kind or another. In the second dream—well, Tom wasn't actually in the second dream. It was about me and the Gentleman, who had found out that I had someone new, even though I'd tried my best to hide it from him. He was very, very angry. Just before I woke up, he was pinning me down on the couch, intending rape, and I was yelling for help as loud as I could.

I rushed home on an early train and met Tom on line at a movie theater on 19th Street, where he had free passes to a new release. He was an expert at getting freebies. For the first, and maybe the last time, we gave each other these proprietary but sort of hopeful looks two people do when they're just getting used to the idea that they're dating, and may not need to go hunting fresh game for a while.

I'd been too busy to eat before the movie, and by the time it was over, I was seriously starving. So I was not altogether pleased when the people in the theater announced that the two men who'd made the film were there to talk about it, and answer audience questions.

Tom was inclined to stay and listen, though he'd have left with me if I'd asked him. Two things stopped me: 1) It was a serious film and I thought the people who'd worked on it deserved a listen, and 2) we were in the middle of the second row, with lots of people to step over if we left. There was no way to be inconspicuous about it.

I didn't mind staying, or wouldn't have, but soon I was so hungry it was actually making me fidget. Tom took one look and knew what to do by some primal impulse that, I imagine, bypassed his brain and went straight from his eyeballs to his fingertips: he started stroking me, ever so gently, on the back of the neck. It worked immediately of course. I stopped shifting around and sat with my spine straight and my head thrown forward. Just keep doing that, I thought, and I'll stay here with you forever. He knew exactly how to touch me: very lightly and slowly, the way you would pet a timid cat, being careful not to frighten it away.

I hope you've enjoyed this up to now because, I have to warn you, it's all downhill from here.

A few years ago, I interviewed a man named Morris

Katz (that's his real name) who's in the Guinness Book of Records as the fastest painter on earth. To demonstrate his prowess, he painted a painting in less than a minute and a half, a snowy scene, titled "Mother and Child Lost in the Woods."

"It's almost done," he said, as he covered the canvas with a layer of white paint. It didn't look that way, but sure enough, it was. That's exactly what it was like with me and Tom: one minute you're preparing the canvas for what seems like something important to come, two minutes later you're ancient history. Sitting there in the movie theater, and at a second Japanese restaurant afterward, all I could see were possibilities opening up before me. And in fact, it was already almost over.

I should confess that I've switched things around: the date at the movies was actually a few days after I came home from the country. I did see Tom the night I came home, but we didn't go to the movies. Instead, we made an appointment to meet at a Thai restaurant Tom knew, or thought he knew, but which turned out to have closed several months earlier. We went to a Chinese place instead (OK, so we liked using chopsticks or something). Then we went back to my place, so he could call his cousin.

Tom had been invited to his cousin's wedding that day, and had been waffling all week about whether or not to go. You know how that goes: he really felt he ought to, and really didn't want to. I had not yet learned that he made almost a religion out of not doing what he didn't feel like doing. So of course, in the end, he'd decided not to go.

"Hi, this is Tom," he said to the cousin's answering machine. "I'm really sorry I missed your wedding. My transmission quit working in the middle of the L.I.E., and I had to wait in the cold for two hours until they sent the tow truck, and by that time I was really cold, and I had to go get some hot soup. So, anyway, sorry. Have a great honeymoon."

I sat on my bed, listening in consternation. Something about this frightened me to the bone. The problem was, I couldn't exactly say what. Show me a person who's never lied

— Prima Materia —

to get out of a social obligation, and I'll show you a person who has no friends or family. So what bothered me wasn't that he lied, it was the lie itself. Something about its plaintiveness, I suppose, maybe the hot soup. The way it demanded sympathy. All I could think was that Edith would never, never allow me a lie like that, and that being the case, I would tend to believe it if it were told to me. Which, of course, only means that I'm naive.

A week after we went to the movies, we met for dinner, and I knew almost right away something was wrong. To begin with, Tom was suddenly finding fault with everything. First, he turned up his nose at a restaurant that had no nonsmoking section. Granted, the law said it should have had, but here was a person who spent his life hanging around in punk rock bars. Then, when we did settle on a restaurant, he complained about every aspect of the food, including, to my amazement, that his chicken parmesan was made with mozzarella. (When I pointed out that anything parmesan is always made with mozzarella, he complained that it was bland.)

Also, he barely touched me all evening, highly unusual for him. Most other times we'd been together, he'd been unable to keep his hands off me. Finally, he announced that he didn't want to spend the night together this particular night. I asked him point blank what was wrong.

"I feel like this has been very rushed," he said. "I realize I'm mostly the one who rushed it. I just didn't realize it would make me feel so uncomfortable."

What was I supposed to say to that? I had no idea. We had a long, uncomfortable conversation—actually, two long uncomfortable conversations—during which he worried that I was fragile and becoming dependent on him. I told him as patiently as I could that he had mistaken my enthusiasm for desperation, that I was neither fragile nor dependent, that in fact I hated leaning on other people and did it as little as I could.

Then I took it one step further: I said that we should

stop sleeping together. This may sound like vindictiveness to you, but it wasn't. I was being practical. Almost from the beginning, something about sex seemed to...well, frighten him is the only term for it. He liked being with me, touching me, kissing me, sleeping with his arms around me, but when it came to actual sexual intercourse, he would often tell me he was too tired. And then, when we finally did make love, he couldn't come.

"Talk to me," I had said finally, after a failed attempt.

"I'm puzzled by my sexual response."

I thought about answering: I'm not. You've been running away from this from the beginning. Something's going on here for you. Something's wrong.

But there are times, I know, when talking about sex is like blowing cold air on a hot soufflé. Besides, I hate talking about it, or during it for that matter, even enough to say things like: no, not there, yes, there, that feels good. Even to say—or hear—the things that would genuinely help.

So I wasn't altogether surprised at all when Tom said he felt things were going too fast. His body had given notification before he himself could. The problem was, that I couldn't roll back the past, I couldn't unfall in love with him. All I could do was make him feel that I wasn't so dangerous after all, which was the point of calling for a sexual moratorium: I figured it would take the pressure off.

He said: OK. Yes to all of it. Fine. I felt like we should have shaken hands on the deal, but we kissed instead, then went our separate ways. Well, I thought. I've done all I can do to make him feel less threatened. Then I sat back to see what would happen.

Here is a game I hate to play: I would wait for the phone to ring. It would, of course, from time to time, but Tom wouldn't be at the other end, and no matter who it was, I'd feel bitterly disappointed. I'd go out for a few hours, and spend half the time speculating that when I came home there'd be a message from him on the answering machine, but there never was. Or then, he finally would call and sound like he loved me too, and I would think it was too early to give up hope. More often, I would wind up calling him myself.

I would try not to, of course. I know perfectly well how this game is played. But then I would think: Well to hell with it. If I have to feel like I can't call him, this is never gonna work out anyway, so I might as well. And then I would. And then he'd be totally blank. Neutral. No affection, no hostility. A white brick wall marked "Post no bills." And I'd resolve to wait next time, no matter how long it took, for him to call me.

This went on for about ten days. Needless to say, I was miserable. I would lie around like a beached whale contemplating how miserable I was. I stultified myself with television and flavored tea, and in between shows, wrote bitter poetry about how betrayed I felt.

Eventually, I discovered two things. The first was what a terrible poet I am. The second thing dawned on me more slowly: that I was miserable in comparison with something else, an earlier state, before I'd met Tom, when I'd been...not miserable. Without the Gentleman, or any other man in my life, I'd nonetheless been, more or less, happy. I considered this further and decided it at least seemed possible that without Tom I would, sooner or later, revert to this condition. The more I thought about this, the less logical it seemed to stay stuck where I was.

So I called him, one last time, thinking that it didn't have to be the last time. All I needed was a simple sign of encouragement from him: a little affection, a little impulse to reach out for me, even if I had called him first. Meantime, I decided to be neutral myself. Totally passive. Let him make a move, if he wanted.

But he didn't. Imagine two white brick walls staring eyelessly at one another across an airshaft. It was the deadest, dullest conversation you could imagine. I didn't say I loved him, he didn't say he loved me. Neither one of us suggested arranging a date. Finally, after a long story about how he'd gotten a parking ticket, and how he intended to get out of it, Tom said, "Well, I guess that's all."

"I guess so," I said.

"I'll talk to you soon."

"No, wait. One more thing."

He waited. I took a deep breath.

"I don't think this is going to work out, you and me."

"Maybe, maybe not," he said neutrally.

I paused, wondering if we should discuss it. The thing is, I didn't really want to.

"Well, OK, then," I said.

"OK."

"I feel like I ought to mail you that toothbrush you left me."

"It's not important."

"OK."

"Take care," he said.

"Yeah, you too."

I got up, fetched the toothbrush in question, and pitched it down the trash compactor chute. Fool! I thought. I could have been the best thing that ever happened to you. You could have learned a lot about love from me, gone on to your next relationship ready to do it right. I lay on my bed, on top of my quilt, staring at the ceiling, waiting to see if there would be a firestorm of emotion. There wasn't. After a while, I got up, went over to a next door neighbor's for a casual chat and a cup of tea. How totally bloodless, I thought. The Gentleman would have been impressed.

I felt odd: lonely, profoundly disappointed, and at the same time pleased with myself. I had refused to let another man make a miserable jellyfish out of me, love or no love. I had said no.

Edith keeps telling me it was never real. That I used to look at him, and refuse to see what I didn't like, the things that should have let me know he was trouble from the very beginning. He had the most amazing ability to ramble on about the most trivial topics. Whether to lift weights or play

– Prima Materia –

racquetball tomorrow. What kind of juice they give you when you donate blood.

Then there was this business about dancing: there had to be lots of space on the dance floor (a rare occurrence in New York City), or he didn't want to dance at all. And so I remember being in yet another Houston Street place with him—this one is lovely and dark, and used to have gourds hanging from the ceiling, and it's a place you probably know about if you like African music—sitting on a small metal fence next to the dance floor. Tom was holding me from behind to help me keep my balance and tapping his fingers on my shoulders in time to the music of the really nifty Ska band onstage.

I thought to myself: This is the most fun I've ever had with anybody, and it may well have been true. But it was also true that I would much rather have been out on the dance floor.

More serious was his proclivity for walking away from relationships. When I met him, he hadn't talked to his mother in two years, or his only brother in two months. He mentioned so many former girlfriends that I once said lower Manhattan was littered with the bodies of women he no longer wanted.

"And vice versa," he replied. "It's littered with my body, too." Sometimes I wonder if that's how he thinks of me, now: one of the many women who didn't want him. I mean, I know it's not that simple, and you know it's not that simple. But does he?

Everything in this story is true. I suppose you had probably figured this much out: that this has been a true story, with the names changed to protect the not-so-innocent, that these things did happen to me, and in the not very distant past, too recently, many would say, for me to be writing about them just yet.

Agreed. I plead guilty to all of it. But I mean more. I mean that not a single word here is a lie, that all the events here literally, physically happened, just as I've described them, and whenever I've taken the liberty of changing a name or a fact, I've notified you of the change. I don't pretend to have been fair; if the man I've called Tom were ever to read this, I'm sure he would argue with a lot of what I've said. I'm sure he would have his own rendition of the story, probably with complaints about me that I haven't even thought of. So I'm not claiming this is the whole truth, just nothing but the truth.

It seemed very important to me to do this for some reason. To break down the barrier between "truth" and "fiction," to prove by doing it that I could tell a story without telling a single lie, without asking you to suspend your disbelief. I thought it would, somehow, mean something. Now that I've done it, I'm not quite sure what.

When I'm writing, I leave myself notes, at the top or bottom of my computer text, often, but not always, set off from the rest by double parentheses. For a long time, the reminder "((the truth will set you free))" was floating at the top of this work. And this was at the bottom:

"No! Don't back away! Glue your eyes to the screen, to the parts that are most painful, most embarrassing, most problematic, most frightening to write. Write from the white heat of emotion, for once, instead of the judgment of distance, and jump, damn you! Learn to jump!"

That was the point, I suppose, for me: facing some of this stuff down. Too many things in life scare me, but I've told you that already. Falling in love scares me, giving myself to another person scares me, and telling the truth about it scares me most of all.

As for Tom, it's now been four months since that last conversation. When I pass bald men on the street, I look at them differently than I did before, but none of them, of course, are ever him. For a long time I stayed away from his neighborhood: the last thing I wanted to do was meet him by accident.

Once or twice, I've toyed with the idea of calling him, sometime when I know he won't be home, just to hear that answering machine message I fell in love with one more time. I can still remember the tune, and maybe I always will.

Sam kept asking me for the longest time after we broke up if I had "heard from Tom lately?" She understood what I had not said aloud, that I was hoping against hope he would figure it out. It wasn't him I was rejecting, but his fear of closeness. That if he had it in him to ask for a second chance, I would give it to him in a red-hot second.

About a month after we parted company, the same Afro-Reggae-Pop band we'd missed the night after we met played a club in my neighborhood, a wonderful, Granola-liberal club where you could always buy a peace button or sign a petition if you didn't feel like dancing. Tom had dusted off his old lawyering skills to help solve a conflict between that club and some friends of his, and had wound up with a free pass in perpetuity. It was, so I thought, a perfect opportunity. He knew I'd be there, he could wander in for free, we could meet again by more or less accident. He didn't show up, of course.

But in my fantasy he walks up to me slowly, and we stare at each other, eyes locked, unsmiling, without saying a word, for what seems like the longest time.

"I hope you know," I say at last, "that you really got to me. I will never forget you. I hope you know that."

And he says...what? Maybe nothing. Maybe all he does is nod, and take my hand. I look up into his face, he looks down into mine. And who knows? Maybe then we dance.

Female Troubles

Marlene Adelstein

Ever since New York Gas & Electric shut him down, Gil got used to pissing in the dark. He claimed to like the taste of warm beer, which was lucky for him since his fridge was shut off and forget about his TV. It hadn't worked since its screen met with Gil's foot three years ago. He said he sat in the dark, smoking at night in his ratty armchair, its springs long since sprung. Personally, I never saw Gil sit still for one little second. Ms. Gilbert, the therapist at my high school, said it sounded like Gil had A.D.D. I forget what that stands for but he was like Ricochet Rabbit bouncing off the walls. He was always on the move, making his rounds, coming up with schemes and plans and hustling anything that wasn't nailed down. You had to be extra careful around Gil. Ma said you could never turn your back on him. She said, "Carla, he'll steal the wax out of your ears!" And personally, I believed her.

Me and Ma lived in a big old wooden house. It was a two-story building with white peeling paint, divided into four crappy apartments. We lived on the ground floor facing the front, the train tracks right outside our window just a few feet away. We had three rooms. A bedroom for Ma, one for me, and a living room/kitchen combo. Ben, who lived in the apartment upstairs from us, was retired and was always home. Next to him was Ma's friend Shirley. And Gil had the apartment downstairs in the back. It was really just one room with a bathroom. He slipped in through our front window one day—he didn't believe in using doors—and introduced himself. He's been slipping in and out of our window ever since.

You might think it was funny that we lived in the absolute perfect place if you wanted to get out of town. Right there on top of the train tracks, next to the highway, so close you could hear the hum of traffic. The Greyhound stopped right across the street and there was a dinky airport a mile away. Planes flew so low we thought they were going to land in our backyard. Every form of transportation right there at our doorstep. But we were stuck. You either needed money to hop on a bus or train or plane or you needed a place to go. I wasn't old enough to drive and I didn't have money or a place to go, either. But as my hero Britney Spears always said, "Don't let go of your dream. It can happen!" so I was still dreaming. But something always burst my bubble. Like Gil. A-number-one dream-wrecker.

Gil used to mooch off Ma something awful. He was always hanging around, stealing her money, her liquor, her cigs. "He'll steal the eyeballs out of their sockets," she'd say. They'd get into these ugly cat fights, screeching at each other, throwing dishes and lamps until we literally didn't have a plate to eat off of. But the thing of it was, they'd fight and then they'd go into Ma's bedroom and get all lovey-dovey. "Make-up sex" is what Ma called it. "More like 'fight-n-fuck'," Gil would say. A half hour later she'd come out of the bedroom looking bedraggled but smiley. Gil would slip out the front window into the blackness of night—he was always doing that even though the front door was right there—and Ma wouldn't see him for about a week or three and then the whole nasty thing would start over again like a bad wash cycle.

I believe Ma and Gil had what Mrs. Gilbert, the therapist at school, called a "codependent" relationship. They fed off each other's craziness. Ma said "Can't live with him, can't live with him." Since I was a kid I was always getting caught in their crossfire and it was never, I promise you, a pretty sight.

Saturday night. August 17th. Ma had put in a double shift at Artie's. In June Artie put in some booths and a few four-tops and started serving up greasy burgers and called it Artie's Bistro, instead of plain old Artie's, as if it were a classy joint. It didn't fool anyone around here, everyone still went there just to get drunk. Ma didn't care what it was called, she needed the job.

Anyway, that night Ma straggled home real tired like she always did after a double header. You'd have thought she'd have been in a better mood since it had been four whole months since Gil disappeared. Everything had been so nice and quiet and Brady-like while he was gone.

Ma was sitting at the kitchen table and said, "Carla honey, I don't like it."

"You don't like what?" even though I knew what was coming.

"I got me one of those feelings. And you know what that means." Some people can feel when it's going to rain. Ma could feel when Gil was near. She had this sixth sense when it came to him. And she'd never been wrong.

Okay, before I go any further you're probably wondering why Ma let that slimy, skanky snake into her life time after time after time. Well, I must admit that is one of those mysteries of life worthy of its own show on the Discovery Channel. I was sixteen, well fifteen, nine and a half months to be exact. Not that old, but old enough to know a few things. I had not been able to figure it out. I'd spent some time trying, trust me. Gil had been slithering around for a long time, since I was eight. Everybody around here called him "the Houdini of Bewilderness." I kid you not! Bewilder-fucking-ness, New York! Gil could get in and out of anything in no time. So it was no use changing a lock or hiding your money. And I hate to admit it but I think there was something about Gil or about their awful relationship that Ma liked. There had to be. "People get comfortable in their pain. It's familiar and sometimes familiar can be comforting. You know what to expect." That's what Ms. Gilbert, at school, said. When I told Ma what Ms. Gilbert said, she yelled, "I don't want you talking about our private home life with no shrink!"

Back to the story. Ma had her feeling, and sure enough Gil slipped in through the window and back into our lives later that night.

– *Prima Materia* –

At first Ma acted all mad and said, "Damn you Gil! Why can't you use the damn door like everyone else!"

"I ain't everyone else, May. You know that." He was wearing his usual, dirty blue jeans. Gil had shoulder length brown hair that was always flopping down on one side of his face, covering his left eye. He'd toss his head off to the side and his hair would go flying off his face. His eyes were cool blue and he had this intense stare that made you feel like he had X-ray vision and was seeing you naked. He was the skinniest thing I'd even seen and had these fat lips. I truly hate to admit this but he sometimes made me think of Mick Jagger or that Steven Tyler of Aerosmith. Usually I forgot that because he was being so snakey but occasionally I'd catch a look of him and be reminded that he looked like a rock star and it would give me a chill. Maybe that's why Ma stuck with him, she pretended she was sleeping with a rock star.

Anyway, he was all "Look how pretty you look, May. I've missed you so much, May. Did you miss me, May?" He walked up behind her and rubbed himself against her backside and whispered something in her ear. He produced this scraggly, no-doubt stolen, bouquet of flowers from behind his back. She slapped him playfully on the rear but she had this shy grin on her face. She took his hand, walked into her bedroom, with him trailing behind her like a damn puppy dog and they closed the door.

I went to my room and they must have been having make-up sex already 'cause I heard grunting and groaning and Gil saying "I'm coming, I'm coming!"

Ma said, "Who the fuck cares? Wait for me."

Then things got quiet so I must have fallen asleep. Later Gil barged into my room waking me up.

"Hey peaches," he said. He was standing at the foot of my bed, shirtless and barefoot, just his jeans on. Gil had a tattoo on his right upper arm of a coiled snake which was perfect, him being so snakey and all.

"Don't call me that," I said all groggy. I was pissed. No one likes to be woken in the middle of the night.

"Hey mermaid," he said 'cause I used to be obsessed with the Little Mermaid but that was like eons ago.

"Gi-il! I'm not a kid anymore."

"Or should I say Brit–ny?" he said in a high-pitched girlie voice. "Oops, I did it again!"

"Shut up!"

"You're looking pretty cute there, Carla. You wearing a bra yet?"

"Gil! Get out of here," I shouted. Gil knew exactly how to zero in and pick on your weak spots, the spots that made you blush or cringe. I *had* just started to wear a bra, one of those little stretchy ones that almost anyone can wear even if you don't have much going on up there. I was still embarrassed about it. All my friends had reasons to wear a bra when they were thirteen.

"I think I see some little peach pits under that top. Maybe the doctor should examine them."

"Maaaaa!" I called out.

Ma appeared at the door. She was wearing her robe. It was tied loosely and I could tell she was naked under it. She was smoking a cigarette. Benson and Hedges. She called them Bennies. I think she thought she looked sexy holding a Benny. The ladies in the ads were always pretty with real nice clothes and manicured fingers, holding a long, skinny Benny. Ma said, "Quit botherin' her, Gil."

"Gil's being disgusting," I said.

"I'm just playing with you, Carla. Jeez, where's your sense of humor? You on the rag?"

I rolled my eyes. "If you said anything funny, I'd laugh."

"Jesus, when are you two gonna grow up? You're like two little kids," Ma said.

"Am not," said Gil.

"Are to," I said.

"Am not," said Gil.

Ma shook her head and walked away.

"Are to," I whispered.

103

"Heh-heh," Gil laughed and his skinny shoulders bounced up and down. He walked out of my room but he looked back at me with his evil grin and winked at me, his shoulders still bouncing.

The next morning was like the Twilight Zone. Get this. Ma was in the kitchen singing! Ma didn't ever sing. She couldn't carry a tune to save her life but there she was standing at the stove singing "Gypsies, Tramps, and Thieves," that she said Cher used to sing. Anyway, she was singing and flipping Aunt Jemimas onto plates. A huge stack of them! They smelled real good, too. Then she remembered we didn't have any maple syrup and yelled out, "Carla, go to the store and buy some Log Cabin, will you? And be fast about it. The pancakes are getting cold."

Gil was actually sitting at the kitchen table drinking a cup of coffee. This kind of thing just didn't happen at my house. Pancake eating. Coffee drinking. Kitchen table sitting. Nuh-uh. Something was up and I was about to find out what real soon. I didn't ask any questions. I took the five Ma handed me. I liked pancakes as much as the next person and figured it would be a long while till I'd see them again. So I ran to the store, bought some syrup and dashed home.

The three of us sat at the kitchen table and ate our pancakes in silence. Ma must have scrounged up some new dishes from the Goodwill 'cause we three each had a plate of our own. Then the weirdest thing I'd ever seen happened. Gil said, "That was simply delicious, May. *Best* goddamn pancakes I've ever eaten! *I* will do the dishes."

It was weird to Ma, too, because I saw her shoot Gil a look like "What the hell got into you?" She didn't say anything. I know she didn't want to jinx it. She just smiled and nodded. Gil took the dishes off the table and plunked them into the sink. He ran the water, poured in a long stream of dishwashing liquid and started to wash those dishes. Then, get this, he started to whistle. I think it was that same "Gypsies, Tramps and Thieves" tune!

It was all too much to believe. I went into my room and got dressed for school. It was Friday, my favorite school day since I had art class and choir. We were making paper maché objects in art. Mine was a huge head of a woman. If there was time I was going to make a huge body, too. There was a knock at my door. This was too much. No one ever knocked on my door. They just barged right in. I heard Gil say, "Hiya Carla. Can I come in and talk to you for a sec?"

Ma was in the bathroom. I could hear the shower going.

I opened the door a crack, which was enough for skinny Gil to slither through. His arms were dripping soap suds. "Yeah?" I said.

He sat on the edge of my bed. "Nice outfit there, Carla. Britneylicious." I *was* wearing a cute new short red skirt and a top that matched perfect. I got it at Target. One thing about Gil, he did notice things.

"What do you want, Gil?" I said.

"Can't I even give you a little compliment? Can't we have a pleasant conversation like a normal family?"

"We aren't a family," I said 'cause it was the truth.

"Didn't we just have a nice Aunt Jemima breakfast like a real family?"

"What do you want?" I said 'cause I was far from convinced.

"I've got a little proposition for you, Carla."

"I knew it. What do you want?"

"A little business deal. You scratch my back. I'll scratch yours."

"What are you talking about? I don't need my back scratched."

"Listen. I need your help today. There's this new business deal I'm into and it's a two-person jobber. Help me out and you won't regret it."

"I've got to go to school."

"This'll only take a few minutes. I'll have you back in time for your first period," and of course, he smiled and 'heh-

— Prima Materia —

hehed' like a dirty old man. What a re-tard! "You'll just miss homeroom," he said.

"Gil, I said no. Sorry, but no."

Gil stood up and walked up to me. Real close. I mean his fat rock star lips were a millimeter from mine. I could feel his breath on my face. It smelled of cigarettes and Log Cabin. "I ain't asking you, Carla," he said in a soft, whispery voice that wasn't nice. It was serious and scary.

I didn't move a muscle. I just stood there looking into his eyeballs, smelling his cig and syrup breath.

"Let's put it this way. I know a little secret of yours that you may not want me to share with your Ma."

Again, I didn't say anything. I wasn't sure what he was talking about but I had a feeling I knew. This wasn't a good development. Gil having something on you was not good at all. He'd use it against you in a flash.

He smiled and did his 'heh-heh' laugh again but no sound came out. Just his mouth opened a little, that grin and his skinny shoulders bounced.

"What are you talking about?" I said.

"Let's just say, someone I know keeps a very personal diary."

"Yeah, so?" I said. I needed to know what particular secret he was referring to. "Someone I know likes to write about 'FWC's."

My eyes flew open. Gil *had* found my diary! The diary I hid in a very, very, very good hiding place. In my closet, way in the back behind all the hanging clothes and piles of shoes and junk, the plumber had to cut a small door in the wall near the floor where he could get at some pipes when we had a big leak. This was last year during one of the times when Gil was AWOL for two months. We never told him about it. The door is very small and if you didn't know to look for it you would never see it in a million years.

But somehow, someway, Gil had found the secret door and found my private diary and read it! I had written about Frank LeMont. He was a guy in my school. He was in the eleventh grade and was kind of cute. Very cute. All right, gorgeous! He was tall and had black hair that kind of curled up a little on the ends. He had this pouty grin that was so sexy and he was just beautiful and very cool. He wore this awesome black leather jacket. It took him months, years, before he even noticed me. And then when he did, he started walking home with me from school and then he used to give me rides in his car and we made out a bunch of times in his car parked over near Lake Lonely in this very private spot he knew. Then two months ago after kissing him for weeks, he said he couldn't stand it anymore. I was too hot and sexy and I reminded him exactly of Britney! Unfortunately, I look nothing like Brit. My hair is brown and wavy. I'm shorter than her and don't have an awesome body like she does. I can't sing or dance. So you might think I'm the stupidest person in the world but kissing Frank LeMont kind of got me going and hearing him say that about me and Brit in the same sentence, well, I was a goner!

He slid his pants off and he wasn't wearing any underpants and his thing was right there. It was huge! I had never really seen one up close like that. Scratch that. I had never seen one, period. Ever. In my whole life. He said, "Go ahead, baby, you can touch my cock, it won't bite you."

I looked into his eyes.

He nodded, "Go on. Touch it."

And I did. And it reminded me of a fat worm. And I wrote that in my diary. I said I touched his fat, wormy cock! FWC, I called it for short! Disgusting Gil had found my diary and now he was going to use it against me. And what's worse is that I wrote about more than just touching Frank's FWC. I wrote about how Frank said he was going to burst if we didn't do it and he'd be real gentle and I was going to love it and he had read how Britney did it with Jason Timberlake before they broke up and it was beautiful and Jason was so kind and gentle and sweet and I said "Where'd you read that?" while I was still touching his thing and he said, "I don't know, somewhere, maybe Seventeen," and I said, "I don't think so Frank" and he said "Shut up, Carla" and put his tongue in my mouth to shut me up. He pulled a wrapped condom from out of somewhere even though his pants were down around his ankles. I heard him rip the wrapper and then things got all confused as he pulled down my panties and there was all this moving around and manipulating as he got me in the right position in the back seat and he got himself up above me. I didn't really know what was going on or what I was supposed to do. I just laid there and let Frank do the work. He grunted the way Gil does with Ma. It didn't hurt that much but it wasn't really any fun. But now I'm not a "V" anymore, that's what I called it in my diary. So at least I got that over with.

Anyway, Gil read all the details and it was certainly not something I planned on sharing with Ma; let's say she wouldn't be too understanding and that's all I have to say about that!

"I'll tell your Ma I'm driving you to school," Gil said then walked out of my room.

Ma stood at the doorway in her bathrobe and waved goodbye to us. Gil must have really sold her a good one 'cause she never waved goodbye to me before. He gave Ma a sweet smile and wiggled his fingers. "Toodle-oo," he said! I sat next to him in his Chevy, a pile of rust that stank of cigs. He drove away in the direction of my school and then cut across Pinehill Road and shot up Route 22 towards Paris, Connecticut which is the opposite direction of school. Bewilderness is a little town in New York near the Connecticut border. All these ritzy people lived in their ritzy houses next door in Paris, Connecticut. But the name Bewilderness totally fit 'cause anyone who lived there was bewildered as to why they were there, how they were going to get out and how they got stuck so close to the rich folk.

I turned to Gil and said, "Where we going?"

"You'll see." He didn't mention my diary again and I wasn't about to bring it up either. If I was lucky, I'd do what he asked and be done with it and Ma wouldn't ever have to find out. <u>If</u> I was lucky.

You might wonder what Gil did for a living. He was not exactly what you'd call employable. He'd had some jobs.

Selling Bibles door to door. Encyclopedias. Last year he was into pay phones. You can actually buy yourself a pay phone, have it installed somewhere like in front of a deli or the Wash-n-Fold and all you do is go and collect your quarters. But between cell phones and the low-lifes who kept robbing his pay phone that was the end of Gil's get-rich-off-people-yapping scheme. Then there was the aerial photo scheme. He had to go door to door and convince people that they needed a photo of their house taken from a helicopter above it. Don't ask me why anyone would want an aerial shot of their house but they did. Gil was also what Ms. Gilbert called anti-social and had problems with authority. So no matter what job he had, he'd end up getting in fights with people and that was that.

Gil's most successful "job" was when he worked funerals. He went around to all the funeral homes and visited the dead people all laid out. He acted like he was their long, lost best friend and would sob over the corpse. While he was sobbing, he was also tugging off wedding rings, watches and any other piece of jewelry that was in the casket. He once took an old lady's orthopedic shoe because that's all there was to take and he didn't want to walk away empty handed. He'd sell the jewelry to Billy Ray's pawnshop. This worked for him for awhile but eventually word got out and the funeral directors knew to watch for him.

Anyway, Ma was always saying that "Gil is creative. If he only could use his creativity for something legal, he'd be rich." Well, I don't know about that. She'd also say "He'll steal the dandruff off your scalp," so go figure.

He drove over the border into Connecticut where suddenly it became picture-postcard pretty. White churches, white picket fences. Everyone's yard was mowed and trimmed and perfect. No trailer parks, no clotheslines hanging out front, no front yards with broken down cars and pick-up trucks. No, Dorothy, we were not in Bewilderness any longer!

He pulled up a long curvy driveway that led to a beautiful house. It was like out of a fairy tale, made of stone and wood and had lovely trees and a garden with all these beautiful flowers in bloom. You couldn't help smiling when you looked at this house. This was a house, I imagined, where only good things happened, Aunt Jemima every morning, home-baked apple pie ala mode at night, flowers in vases in all the rooms.

There were no cars in the drive. Gil hopped out of the car, not even worried at all that someone might be home. "Let's go."

I followed him round the back and kept whispering, "What if someone's home? What if someone sees us?"

"Put a flap on that trap," he said tossing his head so his hair flew off his face.

He walked right up to the back of the house. There was a big swimming pool, a pool house, tennis courts. He motioned with his hand for me to follow close to him. Around the side of the house was a window on the first floor. Gil reached up and wiggled it and the window opened a crack.

"How did you...?"

"Shut up," he said to me.

It was too high for him to reach up and open all the way. I now saw why he wanted me along. He needed another body to hoist up and open the window. And that's what he did. He cupped his hands together and made a little step. He nodded his head again, wanting me to step onto his hands and he'd lift me up to the window. "Gil, I am not going to break into this house!" I whispered.

"You aren't breaking in," he said. "The window's open. Now can it and get up there or Mommy dearest is going to hear about your lovely time with Mr. Fat Wormy Cock."

I shut my mouth and breathed out. I was mad. He had me and there was nothing I could do. I was just grateful he didn't know about the *other* thing. The other thing I was so glad I hadn't written about in my diary. The thing that had me real worried. I hadn't yet figured out how to deal with the other thing.

I stepped into Gil's hands and he hoisted me up. I opened the window all the way. "There," I said and looked down at him.

"Inside," he said nodding towards the house.

He took hold of my ankles and shoved me inside. I landed on the floor with a loud thud. "Goddamn you, Gil!" I said loudly. The room was dark and I figured no one was home. If this house had an alarm system, Gil must have shut it off or figured that out somehow, 'cause it didn't go off.

I stood up and looked around the room. It was painted yellow and was bright and cheery. All the furniture matched and had pillows that weren't the same pattern, but were close and looked fluffy and soft and you just wanted to lay down on the big couch and take a nap. There was a table next to the cushy couch with lots of framed photos. I picked one up and saw a pretty mom with perfect, blonde hair all smiling with her arm around her lookalike pretty, blonde-haired daughter.

I heard Gil shout, "Carla!"

I walked over to the window and saw him standing there with his hands in his jean pockets. "What?"

"Go open the fucking front door! And don't touch anything!"

I went to find the front door. I came to the kitchen which was huge, with gleaming pots hanging over the stove suspended from a big oval rack. Through the glass windows in the cabinets you could see pretty, colorful dishes. Tons of dishes. Ma and Gil would have a field day fighting and throwing dishes in this kitchen. There was one of those islands in the middle with a countertop that was all shiny with little flecks of gold that shimmered. And everything was sparkling clean. Nothing out of place. I never had seen such a clean kitchen! Maybe it never got used.

The living room was gorgeous, too! More comfy-looking couches, huge ones with tons of pillows. A black shiny piano in a corner. Windows everywhere that looked out onto the pool and more trees and flowers. It was a dream house!

I finally found the front door. I unlocked and opened it.

Gil was standing there shaking his head. "What the fuck took you so long?" He didn't wait for an answer. "Follow me," he said.

He obviously had been in this house before. He knew where he was going and headed straight there without glancing at the pillows or the dishes or the paintings or the fancy oriental rugs. I stopped to poke my head into another room.

It was a girl's room and painted all periwinkle! That was my new favorite color not only because the color was so pretty but because the name was so great. Periwinkle! This room had a few stuffed animals but not too many and the most beautiful white wicker furniture. I couldn't help myself and walked in and laid down on the bed. I just had to feel what it would be like to be someone else, a rich girl with fabulous furniture. I looked over to her dresser top and saw a framed photo of that same girl. The frame said "April" spelled out in tiny white buttons. There were all kinds of make-ups and perfumes on the dresser, too. Not the kind you get at Rite Aid but the fancy expensive kind with beautiful bottles or bright packages. I sprayed some perfume on my wrist so I could smell like April. It was sweet and smelled like fresh lilacs. Then I couldn't help myself. I opened April's closet door. I had to see what kind of clothes April wore.

But just as I was about to take out a black silky dress, Gil was standing behind me and yelled, "What the fuck are you doing? I told you not to touch anything!"

"I'm just looking!" I snapped back.

He snatched April's two pillows off her bed and shook the pillowcases until the pillows slipped out. He left the pillows and kept the cases, then grabbed me by the wrist and dragged me off to this other room with a huge flat-screened TV on one wall and books everywhere else in shelves from ceiling to floor. Who could possibly read so many books, I wondered?

Then Gil walked over to the bookshelf and pulled an old book with a black leather cover towards him and the whole wall slid over! It opened into a secret room!

"Wow!" I said. "How did you do that?"

Gil wiggled his eyebrows and smiled. He did his hair-flying head toss. "Magic, huh?"

"No, really. How did you know?" I followed him into the secret room.

"Let's just say I've befriended Maria, the maid" and he wiggled his eyebrows. Then he extracted a key ring out of his jeans pocket. "Voila!" he said and he stuck a little key into a keyhole in one of the walls in the secret room. He turned it and pulled out a long drawer, like a safety deposit box in a bank. He started picking up things from the drawer and tossing them into April's pillowcase. "Here, hold this," he said and had me hold open one of the pillowcases. In he threw all sorts of fancy jewelry, diamond earrings and bracelets, rings, pins, necklaces with sparkly emeralds and rubies, watches, and then stacks of money that were rubber-banded together!

"Gil, you are going to get in so much trouble!" I kept looking behind us. I was sure we were going to get busted.

"Don't worry so much," he said casually. "The alarm's shut off and the little rich family is in the south of *France*." He pronounced it all hoity-toity like *Frohnce*. "They won't be back for months. Believe me, they won't miss these few things. There's plenty more where this came from."

I bit my lower lip. Whenever I was nervous I started chewing on my bottom lip. And I was very nervous now. My heart was pounding like crazy. Not just because I was scared, which I was, but because what we were doing was fun! I felt this amazing rush. Way more than the time Stephanie and I drank about four screwdrivers. I didn't want to get caught now but I didn't want to leave this wonderland, either. I felt like I was in a Hollywood movie, on a film set. No, on *location*, in a real Beverly Hills house!

And right there, holding April's lace-trimmed periwinkle pillowcase open for Gil was the most exciting thing I had ever done. It felt like I was in a movie. I was Brit playing me!

Gil cleaned out the box, closed and locked it. We left the secret room and he shut the door and pushed back the secret book. He glanced around the room and started grabbing other small stuff off tables and cabinets and tossing them into the second pillowcase. A glass candy bowl, silver candlesticks, fancy wooden boxes, and then he found the cabinet with the CD player and gazillions of CD's! With a brush of his arm he swooshed them all into the bulging pillowcase.

I followed him and we headed out. I shut the door behind me. Gil put the pillowcase into the trunk of the Chevy and we got in the car and took off. I watched as April's house got smaller as we drove down the long drive. We drove out of beautiful, peaceful Paris, Connecticut and back into boring, black and white Bewilderness.

Gil dropped me off at school. I went straight to my art class as if nothing strange had happened. I forged a note to my homeroom teacher, Mr. Burnside, who we called Burnbutt, that I had a female problem which made me late. That's what my Ma was always writing in my notes. Nobody ever questioned you when you said you had "female troubles." It was like you could get away with anything in the whole world when you whispered, "I got my period." No one wanted to go down that road.

Anyway, I figured Gil went to Billy Ray's pawnshop to unload his haul of stolen goods. When I got home from school that afternoon, Ma was there watching one of her victim movies on Lifetime for Women and smoking a Benny. She had her feet up on the coffee table, which was an upside-down milk crate.

"Hey Carla honey, how was school today?" More Twilight Zone. She was a little too chipper.

"Fine." I was bursting to tell her about the most exciting day of my life. But I couldn't. Maybe later I could tell Ben upstairs. He didn't talk to anybody but me, so I knew he could be trusted with a secret. When I looked over at Ma, she was looking kind of funny herself. Like she had a secret she was busting a gut to share.

"Are you okay?" I asked her.

She looked behind her, then back at me. "You wanna hear a little secret?" she whispered.

I was right! She sounded giddy. "What is it?"

"Promise not to tell anyone?"

"Yeah," I said. Even though I knew I'd have to tell Ben. I was only fifteen. And I didn't think fifteen-year-olds were expected to keep secrets. Ben was my best friend even though he was sixty. He lived in the apartment above us.

"Your ma might be getting married." And she smiled and then put her hand up to her mouth like a shy girl. I saw she had a diamond ring on her finger!

"What's that?" I said and pointed to her finger.

She smiled again, a big broad one. My ma was real pretty when she smiled and wasn't yelling her head off which was most of the time. When she smiled you didn't notice the dark circles under her eyes or her roots growing in. She had big boobs she liked to show off with low-cut tops, her "best feature," she used to say. I, obviously, wasn't taking after her in that department. It made me sad to think her prettiness was wasted on Gil.

"It's an engagement ring. A diamond engagement ring!" she said. I saw that it was too big for her finger and she had wrapped toilet paper around the back of it to make it fit. "It's real!" she squealed.

"I can see that," I said. Now it was becoming clear. Gil had kept one of the pieces of jewelry and given it to Ma.

"Where'd you get it?" I asked even though I knew the answer.

"Gil."

"You're not seriously considering marrying Gil, are you?" I was in shock. I couldn't believe Ma could be bought off so easily with a piece of jewelry. But more to the point, why would Gil want to marry Ma? "Why buy the milk when you can get the cow for free?" Ma had warned me a million times.

"I know you're not crazy about him, but I think he's turned a corner," she said.

Yeah, I wanted to say, the corner of liar and skank. "What corner?" I said.

"He's got a good job. He's bringing in money. And he's stopped drinking," she said while gazing at her diamond wearing finger. Yeah, right. I saw him drink a beer on the way to April's house that very morning.

"What job?" I said.

"He's in sales at the radio station. He sells air-time for advertisements."

"I don't think so Ma."

"He is really trying this time, Carla. We've got to give him a chance. You saw how good he was this morning at breakfast. He did the dishes! I think he's growing up and ready for a commitment."

How do you tell someone that they are dreaming? I wanted to shout "wake up and smell his whiskey and cigarette soaked breath!" But she wanted to believe it so badly. She must have been having some crazy hormonal fluctuation making her believe these things. She of all people knew the real Gil. Maybe, I thought, she was going through the "change of life" like my friend Stephanie's mom who had dizzy spells, hot flashes and couldn't remember anything.

I knew, though, deep down Ma was what you called an optimist. Beneath all the yelling and screaming and cursing was a woman who really, truly *wanted* to believe. She didn't ask for much.

"But Ma," I said. "People don't change. You've said that yourself. A million times. 'He'll steal the dirt from under your fingernails!' you've said!"

"I know," she said. "I know. I just have a feeling this time. Things are going to be different. It's possible, isn't it? People who want to change, can. Can't they?"

What I hadn't figured out yet was what was in it for Gil? If he promised to marry Ma then there had to be a reason. I didn't have the heart to burst Ma's bubble just yet.

That night I went upstairs to see Ben at his apartment. As usual, he was hanging out his window smoking a cig. Ben was a poet and had a ring of snowy white hair around his head with a bald spot in the middle. He liked to wear red flannel shirts, hang out his window and smoke. "The Thinker," Ma called him 'cause he barely said boo. He was a man of few words but he was a real good listener. He didn't talk to most people but he talked to me. We had great long conversations about all kinds of stuff. The environment and religion and rich New Yorkers and God and culture and poetry and love. Ben was deep. He was the smartest person I knew and my best friend. He gave me great advice and always said, "Carla, you are going places," and he didn't mean I was just going to the mall or WalMart. He meant *places*. In life. Outside of Bewilderness.

I told him everything that happened, from Gil slipping back in our window, to him making me go with him on his "job," to the amazing dream house, the jewelry, pillowcase, April and her perfume. Everything. I told him about Gil finding my diary and I even told him what I said in the diary. And during the whole time I was rattling off this long story Ben just sat there and listened. Then when I got to the end I told him the *other* part. The part that had been weighing on my mind. The part that included stealing three E.P.T.'s from Rite Aid 'cause they're so expensive and the blue and pink and not being sure, then being pretty sure, then being definitely sure. I told him how I threw them into the dumpster out behind the back of our house so Ma or Gil wouldn't know.

Finally Ben stubbed out his cigarette into his ashtray, a ceramic dish I made for him in last year's art class. "You've got to tell your Ma."

"I can't."
"You can."
"No, I can't.
"Why not?"
"She'll kill me."
"She'll yell but she won't kill you."

I didn't say anything. I played with the button on my shirt, twisting it. It was about to fall off. It was hanging on by one thread. I glanced up at Ben, then down into my lap. I said,

"I think I'd like to keep her," real softly.

"Who?"

"The baby. I'm gonna name her April. Or Britney. Or April Britney."

"Carla...," he said in his scolding but patient voice he sometimes used.

"Or Britney April." I rubbed my tummy. "I don't feel her in there or nothing. It's hard to believe I'm actually growing a baby in here."

Ben coughed a few times. He had a nasty smoker's cough but that didn't seem to make him want to quit. He pulled out a white handkerchief from his pocket. He spit into it, then balled up the handkerchief and shoved it back in his pocket. "Carla," he said, "have I ever steered you wrong?"

"No." It was true. He hadn't. Ben had never married. He had been a custodian for years at the Psychiatric Hospital in Dover a few miles away. Ma said that people in town said he had really been an inmate there. They called him names like recluse, hermit, and freak. Sometimes, if he went off his medication he'd disappear for a few days. I didn't care about that shit. To me he was just Ben, my very wise friend who had never steered me wrong. I had to trust him about this, too.

After a few minutes I said, "I heard Frank rip open the condom package but when he was finished I saw the package on the floor and the condom was still in there all folded neat and nice. Could Frank have folded it up and put it back in it's wrapper?"

"No," said Ben.

"Oh," I said. I looked at my hands. I bit my fingernail. I felt stupid. "I didn't think so."

"Don't do it with Frank anymore. Okay?"

"Okay, but..."

"No buts." He lit another cig and took a long drag. He placed it in the ashtray gently. Everything about Ben was gentle and patient and kind. "But if you have to, make sure there's always a rain bonnet on that head. Catch my drift?"

"No," I said. Sometimes Ben forgot I was only fifteen.

"*You* put the condom on the guy."

"Oh."

Then Ben told me that I had to retrieve my diary and destroy the evidence so Gil couldn't use it against me ever again. I didn't want to destroy it. I liked writing in my diary. It was like talking to a friend. So he told me to give it to him and he'd keep it hidden in a good spot. I could come up to his place to write in it anytime, he said. Then he said that Gil must have something on Ma. There had to be a reason why he'd want to marry her.

"That's exactly what I thought!" I said.

"Two can play his game," he said.

Late that night, I followed Ben downstairs right into Gil's room! We knew he'd be out 'cause Gil was part bat, he came out at night like them. He had the same kind of sonar detection skills, too. Gil never bothered to lock his room since he didn't have anything worth stealing. He had no secrets, so I doubted we were going to find anything. Ben brought a flashlight so we could snoop around. Gil's room was depressing. It smelled of sweat and cigarettes. There was a mattress on the floor with dirty rumpled sheets. One ratty chair in a corner and a little table near the window. We opened his closet and saw jeans hanging on hooks, T-shirts tossed on the floor. A pair of tennis shoes with holes. And one brown Ralph Lauren cashmere sweater. Go figure. We opened the kitchen cupboards. Medicine cabinet. Waste basket. Nada.

Then Ben lifted up Gil's pillow and I don't know what made him do this, but he shook it. Out fell a piece of paper. He picked it up and read it.

"Case closed," he said. Then he handed it to me.

It was a bank statement. Ma's. And it showed her bank balance. Ten thousand plus dollars! Ma had money in the bank! I don't know where she got it but surely this would be reason enough for Gil to want to marry Ma. Then he'd wangle his way into Ma's bank account.

On Ben's advice, I took the bank statement to show Ma the truth. I needed to tell her all the news but I had to be delicate about it. When she came home from her shift waitressing at Artie's I sat down next to her on the couch. I waited till there was a boring car commercial on TV then said, "Ma, I've got good news and bad news."

She looked at me funny. "What's the good news?" she said.

"I found out why Gil wants to marry you." I showed her the bank statement and told her how me and Ben went snooping and found it in his pillowcase. At first she didn't want to believe the truth. Ma grabbed the paper and looked at it and then started yelling. Fucken this and fucken that and goddamn Gil and lying bastard. You know, the usual. Then she looked at me and said, "That ain't good news, Carla!"

"Well, it might be better than this part." Then I told her where her diamond ring came from and how Gil made me help him rob the rich people's house in Paris. I begged her not to tell Gil that I told her everything. "He'll kill me."

She was fuming. Shaking her head and going, "He ain't going to kill you. I'm going to kill him first!"

When she finally calmed down I asked her, "Where *did* you get all that money?"

"That was my inheritance from grandma. That's the longest secret I've kept from Gil." She looked me straight in the eyes. "That money, Carla, is your ticket out of Bewilderness!"

I wanted to tell Ma about Britney April, I really did. But I couldn't. I was frozen with fear. She'd done nothing but yell for years about not "giving it up," "keeping my legs closed," and how "all boys want only one thing." How could I tell her? And after she told me she was saving that money for me. How could I disappoint her? Also, I liked having this private, secret thing in my belly. Something that was mine, just mine. Besides, every time I thought about Britney April or April Britney I got this warm, squishy feeling in my belly. A nice feeling. I wanted the baby.

Maybe it was because I wanted something to remember Frank by. Ever since me and Frank did it, he had been ignoring me. I'd walk past him in the hall at school and he'd look right through me as if I were a ghost. I'd say his name, "Hi Frank," and he'd keep walking. He didn't even blink. It was like he was deaf. I called him on the phone and he was never home. He just disappeared out of my life as quickly as he entered it. Every time I thought about that it made me cry. But when I thought about sweet, innocent Britney April I stopped crying.

Anyway, Ma had to wait for Gil to turn up. Who knew when it would be. It could be weeks or months. This time it was two weeks. Ma came home from work and she had one of her feelings that night. "Yup, yup!" she said. "Tonight's the night, baby. Hold onto your horses. It's gonna be a bumpy ride!"

Sure enough, after midnight there was Gil, barely through the window when Ma started screaming at him, waving her bank statement in the air, telling him *she* found it in his pillow, not me. Then she yelled some more about the stolen engagement ring. Gil shot me a lethal look. I ducked out of the way 'cause I knew what was next. Dish throwing. But Ma had been prepared this time. When Gil went to the cabinets for dishes, there were none. I mean literally, the cupboards were bare! Ma must have taken the dishes to her friend Shirley's apartment. So Gil just went straight for Ma. Shirt ripping. Hair pulling. Biting. Gouging. Kicking. It was ugly.

"You whore! You fucking unappreciative whore! I give you a goddamn diamond ring and you accuse me of..."

"You lying scumbag piece of shit. I won't have you lie to me anymore and use my kid for your crimes!"

"Fuck you!"

"No! Fuck *you*!" Ma shouted back.

"Gimme that ring! I want my goddamn ring back!"

"Hell no!" Ma said. But she waved her hand, the one with the diamond ring, in front of his face to taunt him.

"Gimme that ring!" and he was grabbing at her, trying to tug it off her finger. She must have gone to the jeweler to have it made smaller, 'cause that ring was no longer big on her finger. It was on there tight, no toilet paper.

"Over my dead body," she said.

"That's fine with me!" he shouted back. "Where's that whore of a daughter? Just like her whoring mother. The bitch is pregnant. Did you know that?"

"Shut up you...what?" Ma stopped her raging for a second and looked for me.

That damn Gil, he was like the CIA dredging up every known secret to mankind. He must have gone dumpster diving and found my positive E.P.T.'s. He caught me off-guard.

"Is that true?" Ma said.

"Not exactly," I said.

"Heh-heh," Gil laughed his shoulder-bouncing laugh. Now he was enjoying himself.

"Either you are, or you ain't!" Ma screeched.

I looked down at the ground.

"Well?" she yelled.

"I am."

"Jesus H. Christ, Carla! How many times have I told you? Who did it to you?"

"No one you know."

"Who?"

"Frank LeMont."

"Who the hell is Frank LeMont?"

Then Gil piped in, "Tell her about his FWC."

"Shut up, Gil!" I shouted.

"Who's Frank LeMont?" Ma said.

"He's in the eleventh grade." Then I added, "He's gorgeous."

"Well I'm so happy for him," said Ma. "You're knocked up. What good does his being gorgeous do you?"

I didn't say anything. I shrugged my shoulders.

"He didn't use a condom or nothing?"

"I thought he was but then I guess he didn't."

"Holy Mary, Joseph, and Jesus! You don't know nothing! You're too young to be doing this! Jeez!"

"I'm sorry, I'm sorry. Quit yelling." I saw Gil slithering

away. He went to get himself a beer from the fridge and watch the action from the sidelines.

"Quit yelling? Do you know how much abortions cost? Damn, Carla. When are you going to use your head?"

"I'm going to keep her," I said softly.

"What?"

"I'll be a really good mother. Like you. Britney April will be sweet and quiet. She'll be no trouble at all."

"Carla. I'm a shitty mother! You're not having the baby. I'd end up raising the brat and sorry, but I've been down that road before. You're only fifteen fucking years old!"

Then I started to cry. I don't know if it was all the yelling or Ma not wanting me to keep the baby or her saying I was a brat or Gil stealing my last secret. Ma grabbed her lighter and a Benny off the table. She lit her cig and took a long drag. She exhaled and shook her head for a long time. "Go to bed. We'll deal with this in the morning. Shit."

I went to bed and could hear Ma and Gil start up again with another round. They kept at it for a while longer.

I heard Ma scream, "God damn you Gil, if you ever tell me again, 'May, I love you', I'll fuckin' kill you!"

"Not if I kill you first, cunt!"

Then I could hear they were getting tired, winding down. They moved to Ma's room and the fighting turned to muffled talking. I heard Ma's headboard banging against the wall and the bedsprings creaking wildly. They were into the final innings of "fight-n-fuck."

I was lying in bed and I started to think about what it would be like to actually have a baby. A sweet, quiet little baby that didn't talk back, smelled of baby powder and poop. Her tiny fingers and itty-bitty fingernails and soft head. Then I fell asleep.

When I woke the next morning, Gil was gone and so was Ma's diamond ring. He got it off her finger somehow while she was sleeping. Ma was sitting at the kitchen table in her bathrobe smoking a Benny. We looked at each other. She looked tired and I could tell she wasn't going to yell at me

— *Prima Materia* —

anymore. It was like the whole craziness with Gil and Frank was a bad dream that never happened. Even though it had. I knew I'd have to get an abortion and Frank was never going to speak to me again. And Ma knew Gil would sneak back into her life, eventually, to torture her some more. But for right then, it felt like our female troubles had vanished and we could breathe.

Ash Wednesday
An Excerpt from *Saint Thomas' Passion*

William Boyle

I was watching Rensel Downs drink a mixture of what he claimed was three different kinds of whiskey and ginger-ale out of an Atlantic City thermos, as Ms. Pritchard paraded back and forth in the front of the classroom, talking about Anne Frank. Ms. Pritchard was our English teacher. She was also our homeroom teacher and, sometimes, when Sister Roberta, the nun of my and everybody's nightmares, was out sick, Ms. Pritchard filled in as our Spanish teacher as well.

Ms. Pritchard was oblivious to the goings-on in her classroom. Rensel Downs, slugging the fiery whiskey concoction born at the foot of, most likely, his father's liquor cabinet, looked at me and grinned. He had ashes on his forehead. All of us did. It was Ash Wednesday, and there had been a ceremony earlier in the day. The ashes made Rensel look particularly menacing. He took a long drink of booze and shook it off. That devil! He *was* smooth. "Come on, Tommy," he whispered, holding out the thermos. "Put a little hair on your nuts."

The French, an enormous bully who wore a necklace of dirt on his pimpled neck, laughed at this. He sat two seats behind Rensel, head on the desk, drooling; dreaming, I imagined, about hamburgers. He cracked up whenever anybody mentioned nuts. "Tommy's nuts are *bald*," he said. I noticed the ashes on his head. They were shaped like a woman with her legs spread.

I took the thermos with a shaky hand. I looked up at Ms. Pritchard. She was gazing at the floor, going on about brave young Anne Frank. I unscrewed the crusty cap, smelled the stuff, and nearly puked. By now everyone's eyes were on me, even Maria Fagan's. The Wondrous Maria Fagan! Braces on her teeth, breasts beginning to show beneath her white blouse, an ash thumbprint on her gentle brow. The Beauty of the Seventh Grade! How often I thought of her and how I hoped she stared at me when I wasn't looking. Now was my chance: I took a long drink and kept it down. It burned like hell. My classmates sighed and nearly clapped. Forget Anne Frank! This was bravery. This was daring. This was the stuff of heroes.

Before I knew it, silence had befallen my classmates. There was, all at once, a collective gasp. I tried to get the thermos back to Rensel, fearing the worst, but it was too late. A hand reached out and caught my wrist. It was Ms. Pritchard! Awakened after years of dozing! Oh my shit!

"Thomas Heal," she said to me. "What is this?" She held up the thermos and showed it to me. "What is *this*?"

"Oh Lord," I said. I looked at Rensel. I looked at The French. I even looked at the glorious Maria Fagan. She put a stick of gum in her mouth on the sneak. She now wanted nothing to do with me. She chewed and chewed. She rolled her wonderful brown eyes. "Saint Tommy," she said to her girlfriend Stephanie Dirello. "*Stupid* Saint Tommy."

Stephanie put her chin in her hands and giggled. Soon a wave of giggling began. Goddamnit! The misfortune!

I put my head down.

"Thomas Heal," Ms. Pritchard said. "Raise your head immediately! Is this some kind of joke to you? And the rest of you: Quiet down! I've had quite enough."

Everybody shut up fast. Ms. Pritchard had never, in our few months together, raised her voice. Not even when Rensel Downs poured a mixture of orange juice and cockroaches down the shirt-back of Eddie Marino.

"I've had quite enough," Ms. Pritchard said, lowering her voice. She held the thermos up to her nose and sniffed it. She got the whiskey, a nose full of it, and coughed, nearly hacking up a surprised bit of breakfast. "Whiskey?" she said.

"You're twelve years old, Thomas! Whiskey? I CAN'T BELIEVE IT!"

"Oh, Lord," I said again.

"What do you have to say, Thomas? I can't imagine you have an explanation. This is awful, just terrible. What will I tell your mother?"

"My mother?" I looked at Rensel. He looked away, whistled.

The French, all two hundred overwrought pounds of him, leaned forward in his desk, and said, "Tell his mother, Teach! Ha!"

"Oh! Shut up, fatso!" I shouted. "You horse! You fat, terrible thing!" I was getting deeper and deeper into crap. Now, not only would Ms. Pritchard and my mother have my head but The French would also want a piece of the action. He would sit on me. He would rub my face in his belly. Then, as he had once done to the stuttering Chris Caldwell, he would take a bite out of my arm and I would have to be rushed to Victory Memorial Hospital and sewn up and my mother would shake her head and say I got what I deserved and it's a good thing that the Lord didn't see fit to take my whole arm.

"You're dead, Tommy," said The French.

"This has to stop!" Ms. Pritchard cried. "Whiskey! Threats! Jesus, Mary, and Saint Joseph, where am I?"

I didn't understand. Why me? Why, suddenly, had Ms. Pritchard decided to give a good goddamn what went on in her classroom. I had seen Rensel Downs finish an entire pint of vodka, light a cigarette, and put his feet up on Melissa Marotta's desk, looking at a copy of *Hustler*, and Ms. Pritchard hadn't blinked an eye. She had simply gone on talking about Lady MacBeth. "Out *darn* spot," she had said. "*Darn stupid* spot!"

I knew I couldn't fold. I knew I couldn't give Rensel up. I would be a laughing stock, a rat. Maria Fagan would never look at me again. "Ms. Pritchard," I said, "I can explain."

Rensel sat up in his seat. He coughed—a warning that if I handed him over to Pritchard my days were numbered.

— Prima Materia —

"What can you explain, Thomas?" Ms. Pritchard asked. "Whiskey in this thermos? You can explain that? I can't imagine what you've got to say that will explain whiskey in the hands of a twelve-year-old. This is the *worst*! The worst thing I've ever seen!"

"Ms. Pritchard," I said, looking around. Maria Fagan was flipping through her English textbook, doodling in the margins. What was she drawing? My smiling face, surrounded by arrow-pierced hearts?

Ms. Pritchard stepped closer and kneeled at my side. "Thomas," she said, "what do you have to say for yourself?"

Maria Fagan looked at me and gave a half-smile. Was she proud? Did she think me courageous in the face of all this danger? She stuck out her tongue, giggled, and put another stick of gum in her mouth.

"Thomas," Ms. Pritchard said, "what do you have to say for yourself?"

I thought about it long and hard. I examined my hands, creased my brow, and scratched where the ashes were. I began to talk, and then I stopped. I thought about it awhile longer. Ms. Pritchard was growing impatient. Well, to hell with her. An explanation would take time. "Thomas," she said, "I am waiting."

Suddenly, it hit me: My stepfather, Marcos the Terrible. I could set him up for the fall. He was an evil man, a balding Italian who worked in construction. He drank often and was known around the neighborhood as someone you didn't mess with, especially when he had a few drinks in him. I could say the booze was his and that he had given it to me in the hopes of turning me into a man. Genius! Absolute genius! This would take the weight off of my shoulders and, for the time being, put it on Marcos's. If Ms. Pritchard wanted to confront him, let her try. He wouldn't give her the time of day. He was a gorilla. He hardly spoke. He only ate and drank and punched the walls. Ah, Marcos, finally good for something.

"Ms. Pritchard," I began. "The booze is my stepfather's. He gave it to me and told me to bring it to school. He said drinking it would make me a man. He said to pass it around."

Rensel Downs laughed and slapped his desk. Ms. Pritchard's face dropped. "Your stepfather?" she asked.

"Yes," I said. "Marcos. My stepfather."

"I see, Thomas. I see." She got up, went back to her desk, and wrote something down.

I looked at Rensel, who was shaking his head like a wet dog, smiling from ear to ear. "Saint Tommy," he said, "what a friend." He picked up a pencil, tossed it in the air, and caught it. "Here's to Saint Tommy. What a guy." He tapped the eraser against the front of his teeth and laughed.

Being called a *friend* and a *guy* sent chills down my back. I was tough, I hadn't folded, and that was something. Eddie Marino, Chris Caldwell, and even Eugene Biagini, would have folded as soon as mention was made of their mothers. Not me. I was tough. I was no rat. I looked over at Maria Fagan. She seemed impressed. I watched as her elbow brushed across her chest and I felt wonderful.

Ms. Pritchard stood at her desk. "His stepfather?" I heard her say. "That's terrible." A few seconds passed. "Just terrible," she said. She turned and gazed blankly out the window at 23rd Avenue. There were a few cars in the street, a few old ladies humping along the sidewalks with shopping carts. It was gray outside. It had rained early in the morning, stopped for a while, and now looked as if it would start up again soon. Ms. Pritchard turned back to the class. "Just terrible," she said yet again.

It was Ash Wednesday and, on Wednesdays, Ash Wednesday being no exception, we were dismissed early. At twelve-thirty the doors of St. Mary's opened and we rushed out, first the seventh and eight graders, and, fifteen minutes later, for their own safety, the rest of the school, the lowly kindergartners, the overzealous first, second, and third graders,

— Prima Materia —

the dejected fourth and fifth graders, and the awkward, awful sixth graders.

Every Wednesday after school there were at least four fights. The rain, though, had started up again after Ms. Pritchard's English class, in which I had been so memorably busted, probably sometime during Sister Eileen's Math class and, so, many kids went scurrying home to the warmth and dryness of their homes instead of sticking around for the Wednesday afternoon fights. The French and Rensel Downs, however, stayed behind and, thus, I was forced to stay behind. The French had a bone to pick with me and I was not getting away clean. What luck.

We walked up the block and went into an abandoned parking lot next door to Augie's Deli and stood there as the rain began to come down harder. "Saint Tommy thinks I'm a fatso," said The French. "He thinks I'm terrible and fat. He thinks I'm a fatso and I don't bathe."

"I never said that, French," I said, stepping back, putting my hands over my eyes. The ash had washed off of my forehead and run down my cheeks. "About you not taking baths. I never said that."

"You said I was fat and terrible! You're a shit. A rotten little shit!" The French was red in the face. Soaked, he looked angry and sad and somehow fatter. He was a miserable bully, pathetic. In fifteen years I was sure he would be wearing a wispy beard and working as a stock boy in Genovese.

"French," Rensel Downs reasoned, "Tommy's okay. He stood up with Pritchard. He didn't go pussy. He's okay."

"Stay out of this, Rensel," The French warned. "I'm gonna bust Tommy's eye! I'm gonna bust his nose!" The French was serious. He made a fist. He growled. I thought of Maria Fagan, sweet and gentle, walking home in the rain with her knapsack held over her head. What an odd thought to have, I concluded, when another kid, a much bigger kid, is about to bust open your face. I got my guard up. The French drew back and let loose.

It was all over very quickly. Two or three quick shots to the face and I went down like a barrel of lead. The French grunted, spat just to the left of my head, and said, "Punk shit-eater. What a punk." I looked up. The French, pear-shaped, breathing heavily, spat again. "What a shit-eater," he said. "Saint Tommy Heal the Shit-Eater. Some saint."

Rensel Downs shook his head and began to walk away. "He's okay in my book, French, I don't know. You *are* pretty fat. Anyhow, I've got to go. I'm soaked. I hate the rain. It reminds me of crapping in my grandmother's basement bathroom."

The French turned and followed Rensel. He was quiet now, savage. I got up, wiped some blood from my lip, and watched them go. I would have my day, I knew it, and there would be nothing lonely about my moment of victory. I wouldn't pummel The French in an abandoned parking lot in the rain with no one around. I would get him in front of a crowd, in front of Maria Fagan and her girlfriend Stephanie Dirello, on a beautiful, sunny day, and I would make him bleed like no child had ever bled. I hated The French. I had always disliked him but now, suddenly and with good reason, I *hated* him. It felt good to hate him. I laughed the beating off, feeling somehow like I had come out on top, and headed for home.

When I got home, my stepfather was sitting at the kitchen table playing solitaire and drinking a bottle of Taylor's tawny port. He was wearing a flannel shirt with three buttons undone, a gold St. Michael medal hanging in the hollow of his neck, and khaki work pants. His shoes were off and his rough, pink toes were showing through holes in his brown work socks. He took a long drink, coughed into a napkin, and stared at me. "Look at you," he said. "You got in a fight. And you're wet. Soaked." He laughed.

I said nothing. I went over to the refrigerator and took out some bread and cheese. I started making a sandwich.

"A fight. Little Saint Tommy in a fight. How about that? What's the other guy look like? You get him, Shrinkwrap?" He called me Shrinkwrap. It was the worst thing anyone had ever called me; in fact, it was the worst thing I had ever heard. It burned my ears. It stung my heart to hear. I wanted to claw out his godforsaken eyes, strip him down to his St. Michael medal, and send him out into the rain. "A fight, huh?" he said. "Well, I'll be goddamned. A good old-fashioned schoolyard brawl."

"I didn't get in a fight," I said. I finished making the cheese sandwich and took a bite. It was good. I'd been waiting all day for it. I would have preferred to eat it alone, in front of the TV, but the apartment was so small that I had no say in it. There were only three rooms: the kitchen, bedroom, and bathroom, and the TV was in the kitchen, exactly where Marcos had planted himself. Something had to change. The apartment was far too tiny for my mother, Marcos, and me. It had been fine when it was only me and my mother, but she, desperate and lonely after my ridiculous father high-tailed it to Jersey with a waitress from the Nebraska Diner, had to go and get herself involved with Marcos the Terrible and then everything went to the shitter. Once, my mother and I had shared the bedroom. Marcos, of course, complained about that, said it was *unnatural*, and, so, I was moved into the corner of the kitchen, where I slept on a fold-out cot and fell asleep, each night, to reruns of *All in the Family* and the *11 O'clock News*. Unnatural *this*, Marcos. My home life was for the birds.

"You better not let your mother see you like that, Shrinkwrap," Marcos said. "She'll have one of her fits." He took a drink and laughed again. Always with the booze and laughing, this bum.

"There's nothing I can do to hide it. Where is my mother anyhow?"

"She went to Waldbaum's with your Aunt Elaine. Probably to buy you some apple juice. She'll be back soon."

I kept my clothes—I didn't have many, just a few sweaters, T-shirts, and jeans—in a milk crate underneath the kitchen table. I pulled out the crate, went through the pile, and picked out something to wear, a blue sweater and some worn blue jeans. I liked to dress all in blue because it was Marcos's least favorite color. He said blue was for *smurfs* and *fairies*. Might as well paint your toenails, he said. And so I wore blue. And, sometimes, I painted my toenails. I hoped he thought I was a fag in the making. I didn't care about my reputation. I wanted him to hate me as much as I hated him. I finished off my sandwich, took the clothes, went into the bathroom, and changed out of my school uniform.

When I got out, Marcos was shaking his head. "I've been thinking," he said. "We've got to get you your own place. Get you some privacy. Your own room." He laughed and drank, drank and laughed. How dreadful. How hideous. From the entire catalog of possible step-fathers—plumbers from Flushing, electricians from Throggs Neck, schoolteachers from Bay Ridge—how was it that I, an innocent boy from Bensonhurst, who had harmed no one, who tried to be good, who prayed each morning and night, how was it that I had been saddled with this devilish creature, this buffoon, this oaf? Were there forces at work against me? Did the Lord above think it would be goddamned hilarious to see me squirm under the heavy eye of this Italian brute? I said nothing and settled into a chair at the kitchen table. Marcos watched me through the neck of his wine bottle. "Little Tommy," he said, "so fucking quiet."

Half an hour later my mother came home, hauling three bags of groceries. She never came back from Waldbaum's with less than three bags. My mother was a wonderful woman. She worked as an officer manager at a cardiologist's office in Dyker Heights (she was off for the week) and helped out weekends at the church. She was amazing, a saint. In fact, her name being Teresa, many people simply called her Mother Teresa. Some even said that she was better than the *actual* Mother Teresa because what the hell had that old bag done around here lately? Through association, I had gained a nickname that I would never, it seemed, manage to evade: Saint Thomas. Everyone from Rensel Downs and The French and Maria Fagan to Marcos the Terrible and my pitiable aunts and uncles called me Saint Thomas or some variation thereof. Saint *Tommy*. Saint *Tom*. Saint *Tom-Tom*. Whatever. Anyhow, my mother was a saint, and I suddenly feared the call that I knew would be coming that night from Ms. Pritchard. I feared it because I knew it would upset my mother, not only the whiskey part, but the whole lie about Marcos having given it to me. She was, for some reason or another, very protective of Marcos, much as, I imagined, the *actual* Mother Teresa was protective of the diseased and the dying. I helped my mother with the grocery bags and she patted my head. Marcos, still sitting at the table, not even having moved to urinate, said, "Oh, Teresa dear, it seems Little Saint Tommy Shrinkwrap got into a fight today."

The fight had slipped my mind. I felt the bruises on my face and grimaced. Thanks a lot, Marcos.

My mother kneeled down and examined me. "What is this about a fight?" she asked.

"Nothing," I said.

"Now, Tommy, don't you lie to me."

"Nothing."

"A fight, Tommy. You've got bruises. Tell me."

"Nothing happened."

"Was it that awful Henry? Did Henry do this to you?" Henry was The French's real name. The only people who knew and used it were adults, mostly mothers and teachers, and it was always preceded by some very useful and fitting adjective: *awful, evil, cruddy.*

I thought about it for a while and decided to keep my mouth shut. I hadn't named names earlier and it wasn't a good idea to start now. If I gave The French up and my mother called his mother and his mother told his father, who was a retired eater of fire and a lifter of all things heavy, then The French would catch a beating at his father's hands and I, in turn, would not only have no credibility in the classroom, and be in the same league as, for example, Chris Caldwell and Eddie Marino, but would also receive a beating three times as bad from The French and, quite possibly, some of his tougher-than-thou *compadres*, Nick Tuttles, Evasio Moricone, and maybe even Rensel Downs. There would be more blood, puddles of it, my blood, and it would not, afterward, be uncommon to find my teeth in the abandoned parking lot, buried under a half-inch of dust. "It's nothing," I said to my mother. "I fell down in the schoolyard. I tripped over Chris Caldwell's knapsack." Good one.

"Are you sure you're okay? There was no fight?"

"No fight," I said. I looked at Marcos and grinned.

"Okay, Tommy. Okay."

My mother and I put the groceries away in the cupboards and the refrigerator while Marcos simply sat at the table, slugging his port, humming Sinatra. What a bastard. "I'm cooking steak for dinner tonight," my mother said, "and mashed potatoes."

"G-Good," Marcos said, suddenly very drunk.

"I really wish you wouldn't drink so early with Thomas around, Marcos."

"The kid's a fighter. He can take it."

"Really, Marcos. It's not right."

After that, there was silence for a while. My mother and I sat down at the table with Marcos and turned on the TV. We watched a talk show, then the news, then my mother turned off the TV and talked about her day, all the *crazies* she and Elaine had seen at Waldbaum's, the traffic on Bay Parkway, how nice it was to have the week off from work. She asked Marcos how his day had been and he said fine, then he hummed some more. Marcos had also had the day off from work, for whatever reason, which explained why he was home so early. My mother asked me about my day and I shrugged. "Okay," I said. I knew the dreaded Ms. Pritchard call was coming soon.

— *Prima Materia* —

At six, we sat down to dinner. The steak was fine and the mashed potatoes were creamy. I drank three glasses of apple juice. Marcos knocked off the bottle of port and started in on another. He always kept three cases on the floor of the bedroom closet. The man at the liquor store, Mr. Eldridge, loved Marcos. He sent him a Christmas card each year and on every other case of port he didn't charge tax.

"I really wish you would lay off the wine until later, Marcos," my mother said, tapping her fork against the plate.

"You could use a glass yourself," he said, taking a slug. "Take the edge off, you know? You don't have to work tomorrow. Drink up."

"Smart mouth," she said. "Keep it up."

He laughed and drank some more. "Mother Teresa," he said and he shook his head. "Married to goddamned *Mother Teresa*."

"I'd appreciate if you didn't curse in front of my son."

I looked up at Marcos with his wine and at my mother, a single strand of hair hanging over her face. She kept blowing it away. It kept bobbing back down. Then the phone rang. My heart rose. This was it: the *call*. I readied myself for what might follow. My mother would look at me with her sad, holy eyes. Marcos would take off his belt, I knew, show it to me, pound it into his hand, and then come at me. Oh Lord! Why had I taken that damn whiskey at all? Shitty Rensel Downs and his shitty whiskey. Next time I saw Rensel, I thought, I was going to flatten his face with a baseball bat, pin him up against a wall and show him what a beating was.

The phone rang again. Marcos went for it. Shit of shits! Why him? Why not my mother? Why had fate, yet again, stuck out its foot and tripped me? "Hello," Marcos said, sounding almost sober. "What? Yes... What? Yeah, she's here... Hold on." He handed the phone to my mother.

"Who is it?" she asked him, holding a hand over the receiver.

"Shrinkwrap's teacher. She says there's a problem. Probably about his little *tussle*. Ha." Marcos nearly leapt for joy. He picked up the wine and took a long stiff one. Evil fucker.

I looked down at my plate, my face hot and red.

"What is this about, Tommy?" my mother asked me. "Is this about a fight?"

I shrugged. Better not to say.

My mother put the phone to her ear and spoke. "Hello," she said. "Yes, hello, Ms. Pritchard... What's that?... Sure I do, yes... Oh well, that's nice of you... No, I had no idea... What's that?... What?... No... I can't..."

Oh crap.

"He was what... From who?... That's what he told you?"

My mother was looking at me, I knew, even though my head was down. I could feel her eyes burning holes in me. If I looked up that would be it. I'd either have to turn and make a run for it or break down crying. Those were my only two options. This was bad, even worse than I might have imagined.

"Okay, Ms. Pritchard," my mother said. "Yes... I'll take care of it... Okay, we'll speak tomorrow... Yes, thank you." My mother hung up. There was silence. Now, if I looked up, I feared that she might be the one weeping.

"What was it about?" Marcos asked. "The fight?"

"Yes," my mother said. "The fight. He got into a fight." She pushed away from the table, got up, and went into the bedroom. It was the last I saw of her that night.

Later, as I sat on my cot reading about Anne Frank by the light of the TV, I wondered about my mother's reaction. I had expected tears, yes, but for her to turn and walk away and not show her face again all night? This was a punishment indeed. My kind of punishment perhaps on some level, no angry words spoken, no declarations of disappointment, no belt marks on my ass, but its roots went deeper than that. It was the kind of punishment that ate away at you. I knew I wouldn't

— *Prima Materia* —

sleep a wink that night or any until my mother (and, once word was out, Marcos) confronted me.

Marcos, watching a rerun of *Cheers*, was well into his third bottle of port as I struggled with my reading. The light was dim, the canned laughter coming from the TV was intrusive, my mother was in her bedroom thinking about how bad I had turned out, and Anne's story was getting me in the heart. "You really pissed off your fucking mother," Marcos said to me.

I said nothing, kept reading.

"She's in there right now, pissed off," he said. He laughed, took a drink, went back to his show. "Pissed off, brother, let me tell you."

I put the book down. My poor mother, I thought. What had I done?

The Score

Alison Sloane Gaylin

"I can get you some marijuana."

Janet was surprised at how easily the words fell from her own mouth, as if she went out and got marijuana for people three or four times a week. As if they sold marijuana at the A&P, behind the counter with the chewing tobacco and the lottery tickets, and all a person needed was legal proof of age.

As if, on a more practical level, Janet had any idea where to get marijuana these days. The last time she'd smoked it had been thirty-one years ago, as a freshman at SUNY Albany, with her roommate—a slender, halter top-wearing girl named Neruda, who had left the room during the third straight minute of Janet's coughing fit, slamming the door behind her.

But there, Janet had said it, and there was no taking it back. The words echoed in her head. I. Can. Get. You...

"Sounds great," said Steve.

"It does?"

Steve smiled, and Janet noticed his teeth were still white, white as they'd been at seventeen, when he'd washed her parents' windows for extra cash, wearing only cut-offs, his blond curls gleaming in the sun like Alexander the Great in her history book, making twelve-year-old Janet feel the heat of a thousand Persian deserts.

To Janet, Steve would always be shirtless and gleaming and seventeen and needing extra cash. Even at fifty-five. Even with cancer.

~

– Prima Materia –

Janet had lived in Leeds, New York her whole life. Steve, who'd lived in six or seven major cities around the world, had come home to die. At least, that's how Janet's mother had described it, over the phone the previous day.

"Steve Reynolds has come home to die, my darling," Janet's mother said, her voice brittle and mysterious as an ancient shroud.

Janet's mother was very dramatic. She'd even named her daughter after a movie star. Janet's full name was Janet Leigh Clark. She'd never thought much about it, until her parents had taken her to see "Psycho" at a second-run movie theater in Albany. "I can't believe you named me after an embezzling hussy who gets murdered!" fifteen-year-old Janet said, as soon as they left the theater.

"It's only a role, Cookie," her mother said.

"Where do you kids learn words like hussy?" said her father, which caused Janet to roll her eyes so far back into her head she felt car-sick.

~

Janet had been teaching biology at Leeds High for the past twenty-five years, and none of her students knew whom she was named after. Some of them didn't even know her first name. She was Miss Clark, and unlike her namesake, she dressed solely for affordability. She couldn't see the point in spending a lot of money on clothes when specials at The Discount Countess covered her up just fine.

"You have the most gorgeous eyes. Why don't you get contacts?" her best friend Alice would say.

"These glasses were only ten dollars," Janet would answer.

Alice taught Mass Media and Twentieth Century History at Leeds High. She was the type of teacher who'd go out for coffee with her students, take them to foreign films, and say things in front of her class like "In effect, the Viet Cong were telling us to bend over and spread 'em."

Janet was not that type of teacher.

"You know what the kids call you behind your back?" Alice had said to her once, in the faculty lounge.

"Wha-a-a-t," Janet asked, as if she was easing herself into scalding water.

"Clark the Narc." Alice took a Kleenex out of her purse and blew her nose. It so perfectly punctuated the phrase—a sort of audible exclamation point—that Janet wondered whether Alice really needed to blow her nose, or if she'd faked it for dramatic effect. Then, she wondered if her dramatic best friend and her dramatic mother weren't giving her a skewed picture of the world, especially since the death of her father—a man who never opened his mouth when he smiled, but saw the world so clearly, he couldn't help but illuminate it for others.

Then, she wondered why she invited these people into her life: her mother, who wouldn't leave her house but spent at least five hours a day on the phone; Alice, who had been dying her hair goldfish-orange since high school; her ex-husband, Burt, who had vanished from their home after a perfectly pleasant month of marriage, leaving behind nothing but his wedding ring, placed on the closed lid of the toilet seat.

Janet watched Alice purse her orange lips together, lips she'd painted to match her hair, and remembered what her father used to say about her. *There's more coming out of that girl's mouth than there is going on in her head.* "What's a Narc?" she asked.

~

Janet stood on the porch of the house that used to belong to Steve's parents when they were alive, holding the blackberry pie she'd baked him, tight as a talisman. It was late in the summer, and the air around her was motionless and hot, but the pie was hotter still. She felt its warmth

— *Prima Materia* —

through the cardboard box as if it were a living, breathing thing.

"You can really get marijuana for me?" Steve was so thin she could make out the hinge of his jaw, working as he spoke. She wished he would eat, but he wouldn't, he couldn't. "I mean...not to look a gift horse in the mouth, but where would you...I mean, how would you know where to..."

"I have my sources." *I have my sources?*

"Well," he said. "If it isn't too much trouble, I've heard it can do wonders for the pain."

"Not to mention the appetite. I saw a report about it last night on *60 Minutes*. Of course...I...already knew... all about it."

Steve smiled again. Janet would have swooned if she didn't think it would look moronic on a fifty-year-old in a pale peach polyester shirt with brown starfish all over it.

So instead, she watched him. Took in his ghostly body and his gentle brown eyes, the dark hollow of his throat and the Yankees cap, stuck tight over where his curls used to be.

"You're going to be all right," said Janet. "All you need is to get your strength back."

"The way you say it, I believe you."

"Okey dokey then. I'll be back tomorrow with a pound of marijuana!"

"A *pound*?"

"Is that enough?"

"Are you sure you want—"

"There's only one thing I want, and if it takes one or ten or twenty-five pounds of marijuana, I'm prepared to get it." Janet removed her glasses and watched his thin face go all velvety, like that of an aging movie queen, photographed by a kind director. "What I want, Steve Reynolds, is for you to eat my pie."

142

With that she turned and left his porch, intending to take the pie home, freeze it and bring it back—like an A-plus—once his appetite returned.

It wasn't until she'd reached her own door that she once again considered the practicality of it all. Where exactly was she going to get illegal drugs?

But this time, she could see the answer in front of her, clear as she'd seen the bones in Steve's face.

Buy the drugs from Alice's son.

Immediately she had misgivings; Alice didn't know her son smoked marijuana, let alone sold it. For all her gaudy hair and her potty talk in front of her students, Alice seemed to have a blind spot for Shane's pinkish eyes and prodigious appetite, a deaf spot for the gossip that regularly migrated through the faculty lounge. "Boys will be boys," Alice would say, upon noticing her son had cleared out her frozen pizza supply in one afternoon.

Shane is not a boy. He's a twenty-five-year-old, unemployed man who still lives with his mother and smokes a boatload of marijuana! Of course, Janet had never actually said that. But sometimes she wanted to. The times Alice would talk about how little Janet knew of the "big, bitchy world," for instance.

Janet packed the pie in Tupperware and put it in the freezer, between the stack of Chowtime for One Frozen Dinners and the fifteen boneless, skinless chicken breasts she'd found on sale last May at the Super Kmart.

Her kitchen was immaculate, save her Calphalon pot, which had been soaking up dishwashing liquid in the sink for more than twelve hours. In an effort to make Steve's pie as sweet and rich as possible, Janet had reduced the filling for so long that blackberries had cooked right into the stick-proof bottom. The Calphalon pot had been a wedding gift from a spendthrift friend of Burt's. Janet never would've spent so much money on a kitchen utensil, but she did like using it—so much it embarrassed her a little.

Janet spilled out some of the bubbly liquid and went at it with a sponge. The inky stains refused to budge, though, and she feared that no matter how long it soaked, they would persevere.

"My pot is changed forever," she said out loud. *My pot.*

Janet plucked up the receiver of her Mickey Mouse phone (a whimsical, fortieth birthday present from her mother) and dialed Alice's number.

~

"Ummm... My mom's not in right now?"

To Janet, Shane's voice sounded exactly the way it used to in her biology class. (*'Shane, could you explain to everyone what a mitochondria is?' 'Ummm... I didn't exactly read the chapter?'*) She tried to push this association out of her head. Thinking of Shane as a former student made her feel corrupt and power-addled.

Of course, it was Shane who had the power, not Janet. Shane was Purveyor of Desired Goods. He was the one to say yes or no—and, if yes, when Janet could receive the goods and how much they'd deplete her checking account. (Did one write checks for this kind of thing?) He could ask her why she wanted marijuana. He could say, 'Gee, Miss Clark, don't you know drugs are illegal?' He could say, 'Does the principal know you're breaking the law?' He could say anything he pleased, and it made Janet feel angry enough to get the next few words out. "Totellthetruth, Shane. I wanted to talk to *you*."

"Me?"

Why must he turn every statement into a question? To steady herself, Janet dug her fingernails into the palm of the hand that wasn't holding the receiver. "I think there's something you might be able to help me with."

"I might be able to help you?"

God! "Did you, by any chance, watch *60 Minutes* last night?"

"Ummm..."

"I need marijuana, Shane. It isn't for me. It's for a friend. A dear friend who has cancer and could benefit from marijuana's analgesic qualities, not to mention what it could do for his appetite. He's very thin, and needs to put on weight immediately so he can heal enough for a remission."

She felt as if a long, high fever had finally broken—so powerful was her relief at saying the words, so cool was the sweat that trickled down her ribcage and settled into the waistband of her all-cotton briefs.

Janet took a deep reward of a breath that seemed to wash out her insides from top to bottom—*from stem to stern* as her father would've said, having served—quite proudly—in the Navy during WW2. (Interesting, Janet thought as she breathed, that *stem* was both a nautical and a botanical term, and it was a botanical product she'd requested. Interesting also, how similar the word *nautical* was to the word *naughty*.) It wasn't until she'd finished exhaling that she noticed the dial tone on the other end of the line.

~

Janet raked the sponge round the interior of the Calphalon pot until her wrist began to ache. Why had she chosen to make a blackberry filling—dark and viscous as a mortal wound—when there were so many fruit fillings more hospitable to non-stick surfaces?

She poured more dishwashing liquid into the pot, grasped the tip of the sponge between her thumb and forefinger and attempted to erase the stains like pencil marks. It didn't work. She'd probably have to use steel wool on this mess, and then she could forget about the non-stick surface, because it would be dead, cause of death

— *Prima Materia* —

fatal laceration by an SOS Pad oh Dear God in Heaven, why had she called Alice's son?

Janet threw back her head and cried out, *"Why? Why? Why?"*

"Miss Clark?"

In nearly the same thought, Janet realized that 1) She'd forgotten to lock her kitchen door, and 2) Shane was standing right behind her.

She whirled around, and indeed, there he was. Broad-shouldered, thick-waisted Shane Gardner, his long hair limp as old socks, his face doughy from relative youth and too many frozen pizzas. He was wearing huge camouflage pants and, on his T-shirt, a comic book character with a bullet hole between his eyes. Shane was too old to be dressed this way. "Sorry I had to hang up on you like that, Ma'am, but it isn't cool to say marijuana over the phone."

Janet's eyes went from Shane's to those of the gunshot victim. "Oh," she said. "I didn't know."

Shane grinned. "No worries! Just remember, in the future, say *tickets*. I'm interesting in buying some of those *tickets* you have."

"Tickets."

"Right." He made a silly, mime-like gesture with his hands. "You know, the walls have eyes. Or...ears, I guess... Whatever."

"Okey dokey then. I'd like to buy a lot of...tickets. How much is a lot, and how much will it cost?"

"Well, I charge $80 a quarter, but a quarter isn't a lot. You're talking about a sick dude, I'd go with at least a half, which I'd give you a discount on since you used to be my teacher, making it $150."

"All right. It seems expensive but... Do you take checks?"

"Well, see normally I do. I normally have people write *tickets* on the little memo line, but..."

"I can do that."

"No, you can't."

"You won't take my check?"

"I can't sell you any."

Janet's stomach contracted.

"Because—"

"I'm not buying this stuff to go to an...an Eagles concert. *This is for cancer!*" Janet's voice was clear and startling, like breaking glass. She'd only used this tone once, when she'd seen an upturned tack at the exact center of her desk chair. *Which one of you did this,* she'd said, angered not so much by the tack itself, but by the painstaking accuracy with which it had been placed.

"I...I just meant... I don't have any right now, Miss Clark. You can get it from my buddy Israel. He lives on Front Street. I can write his address for you. I'll let him know you're going there, so you can buy it tonight."

"Front Street? Can't I go during the day?" Janet directed the question to the bullet casualty on Shane's shirt.

"He works days. And you gotta buy it fast or he'll smoke it up. Israel's a total pothead, Ma'am."

What was she doing? More accurately, what did she think she was doing? Steve Reynolds had lived on a houseboat in Thailand. He had a twenty-six-year-old son in New Zealand, a thirty-year-old daughter in Cambodia and five-year-old twins in London. He'd written copy for a Parisian advertising agency *in French*. The most exotic thing Janet had ever done was own a Siamese cat. (A whimsical, thirty-fifth birthday present from her mother. It disappeared the following Christmas.) And now she was supposed to visit a pothead named Israel on Front Street at night? Front Street didn't even have lights.

Shane was writing Israel's Front Street address on the small chalkboard that Janet had stuck to her refrigerator to keep track of appointments and groceries. Janet loved the knock of chalk on slate—so quietly authoritative. It used to be her favorite thing about teaching, until the school bought those new, white boards with the erasable pens that squeaked.

"Want me to make you a map, Ma'am?" Shane drew crooked lines and childlike houses on the chalkboard. Next to one house, he wrote "Rick's Ribs" with an arrow, and Janet remembered how she'd gone there, with Alice, on the night of her eighteenth birthday.

"I'll have a beer," she'd said, choking a little on the words. Janet was wearing jeans and an embroidered Mexican blouse that Alice had lent her. She felt as if every male eye in Rick's Ribs were a magnifying glass, burning holes into that blouse, and grasped, for the first time, the power of her youth. She wasn't sure she liked it.

"You know who you look like?" said the bartender. "Laurie from the *Partridge Family*."

"Don't you want to see my ID?"

"S'okay baby."

"But I'm eighteen. Today."

"Happy Birthday, Janet Clark." Janet recognized the voice before turning around. He lived in Hawaii now (a professional surfer, according to the Leeds grapevine) but she thought she'd seen his red Mustang parked outside the dry cleaners, and just this afternoon her mother had verified it. Steve Reynolds was back in town, but just for a few days.

His hair was longer, his skin more tan. He wore a white T-shirt that Janet found herself envying. "Long time no Steve." Janet's cheeks burned red. She wished she could turn her face inside out. "I mean *see*. Long Steve no—"

"You look great."

"Hell-ew," said Alice, in the fake British accent she always used with cute boys.

"This is my friend Alice."

"From Livah-pool."

Steve placed his bottle of beer on the bar. "Want to go to Manhattan?" Golden brown, his eyes were. A hint of candle flame, just around the pupil.

"Manhattan?"

"We can hear some jazz, drink champagne, watch the sun rise over the East River."

"But...New York's three hours away."

"I'll drive." The red Mustang was a convertible.

"My parents—"

"You're going to college, right?"

"Yes..."

"It starts in two weeks. What are they going to do, ground you?"

"Get the fuck out of here and go!" said Alice in her real voice. "I'll call your parents."

Steve smiled, and then he winked, which was like a one-two punch in Janet's solar plexus. "Live a little," he said. "You'll never turn eighteen again."

~

"Israel's in Kingston."

Janet stared at Shane, her mind so flooded with images of Rick's Ribs and Steve Reynolds at twenty-three that it took her several seconds to comprehend the sentence.

Shane was hanging up her Mickey Mouse phone, which he had used to dial the cell number of his friend the marijuana pusher. *Israel is in Kingston.* Not a geographical misstatement from a pudgy dope fiend. Information, derived from the call. "He's where?"

"He works at a nursing home in Kingston three days a week. He says he gets off at midnight, and you can meet him in the parking lot. I got directions for you." Shane erased Front Street, erased Rick's Ribs. Janet wanted to slap him across the face.

Put it back, she wanted to scream, until he had no choice but to do as she said and put it all back—Rick's Ribs, her eighteenth birthday, Steve's sun-drenched hair. But Shane was drawing a new map now, one with an interstate highway, and Janet knew she was thinking irrationally. "Kingston's an hour away," she said.

"Actually, without traffic? It's more like forty-five minutes."

Janet looked down at her thick, beige, Wrinkle-Proof skirt ($15), her Hanes No Nonsense Pantyhose in Sand (five pair for $12), her white Keds ($18, ten years ago) planted on the bright yellow linoleum. "Long time, no Steve."

"What?"

"Nothing."

~

Janet didn't exactly know what one wore to purchase drugs in nursing home parking lots at midnight, but she was sure the starfish shirt, the beige skirt and the Keds weren't it. It was 9:30 PM, and she had been staring silently into her closet for at least fifteen minutes.

She'd spoken to three people today—Steve this morning and Shane, of course, and her mother who had called Janet at five in the afternoon to say, "I think I've broken my hip." (Janet had dutifully hopped into her Chevy Cutlass and sped to her mother's house, only to find the tiny, seventy-nine-year-old woman bent over the stove, basting a roast chicken. "Oh, hi Cookie. False alarm. Taste this stuffing and see if it's too dry.")

That was more conversation than Janet was accustomed to at this time of year. So dreamlike were her late summer days, so deathlike. Whole days coming and going with Janet barely opening her mouth to speak. Summer school was over, real school had yet to begin and, yes, there were the daily phone conversations with her agoraphobic mother, there were the pleasantries exchanged with supermarket check-out clerks or the nice young man who worked at the video store. Occasionally there was iced cappuccino with Alice, but most of the time there was nothing but still heat and silence. By the time Labor Day arrived, Janet's throat would be dry from lack of talking.

Today she'd spoken to three different people and later she'd be speaking again, to a pothead in a parking lot. But as she stared at all the stiff skirts and shirts and slacks in her closet, at those synthetic fabrics that scraped the skin, at those colors found in nature, but at the wrong end of nature, the colors of mud and rust, of rotting tree stumps and decaying flesh, Janet felt so desperately lonely, as if the silence in her room could eat her alive and no one would know about it until after Labor Day.

"What happened to me?" she said to her closet. "I used to have *jeans*. I used to wear *cotton*."

Janet walked to the full-length rococo mirror in the corner. (A rather cruel, forty-fifth birthday present from her mother, given three months after Burt had walked out, along with a card that read, "How do *you* think you look?") For a few moments, she stared at her reflection.

God, what Steve must have thought this morning.

Janet removed her glasses, watched her face soften in the mirror. She wasn't an ugly woman, but she certainly acted like one. Even on her wedding day, she'd worn a charcoal-gray suit that hung practically to her ankles. (Why should she bother with white at her age? she'd thought. Why should she bother with flowers, or make-up, when Burt so clearly loved her for her large, tidy house and her grandmother's meatloaf recipe?)

On page 42 of the biology textbook, there was a series of black-and-white photographs marked "The Stages of a Chrysalis." Janet felt as if, somehow, she'd gone through those stages in reverse. She'd entered Rick's Ribs a butterfly in a Mexican blouse, and she'd come out...she'd come out...

Janet's eyes were a bright, Caribbean blue and her cheekbones were quite good and she still had those freckles on the bridge of her nose, yet she hid it all behind black plastic-framed glasses that looked like something you'd

— Prima Materia —

find in a medical supply store. *Of course* they were only ten dollars. Who'd pay more for them?

She pulled the pins out of her bun, let her silver-streaked, brown hair fall to her shoulders. "How do *you* think you look?" she asked her reflection. Then she called Alice.

~

It wasn't until the two women were in Janet's Chevy Cutlass, headed south on I-87 to Kingston, that Alice began to ask the difficult questions.

She'd been asking easy ones ever since Janet had summoned her to her house, questions like: "Why do you want to borrow my clothes?" ("I have an important meeting in Kingston tonight, and I need to look casual," Janet had replied.) "Do you want me to go to Kingston with you?" ("No. I mean, yes. Yes please!") "Should we take my car?" ("No. It's *my* meeting. And if anything happens, it should be *my* license plate that gets tracked.") "What are you talking about?" ("Nothing.") "You're turning red—why?" ("I don't know. Maybe it's a virus.") "Is that Shane's handwriting on your chalkboard?" ("Of course not! When did you become so paranoid?")

But sitting in the front seat next to Janet—to whom she'd donated her favorite black tank top and a pair of tight, faded Levi's "guaranteed to take twenty years off the ass"—Alice seemed to grow more curious by the mile. "Who," she said, "are you meeting in Kingston at midnight?"

Janet stared straight out at the highway.

"Why won't you look me in the eye?"

"I hope we're not late."

"Why won't you answer my questions? Why are you being so fucking mysterious all of a sudden?"

Janet sighed loudly, hoping it might suffice as a response.

"All right, I'm getting tired of this. Where are we going and why are we going there, and if you don't answer me right now, I'm taking out my cell phone and calling your mother."

"Don't do that."

"Why shouldn't I? I'm sure she'd appreciate knowing her daughter is driving down an interstate highway in the middle of the night with her clavicles showing."

"Honestly, if I'd have known you were going to be—"

"I have her number on my speed-dial, so this'll only take about one and one half seconds."

"Put the phone away!"

"Ready, aim…"

"I can't tell you because it's for your own protection."

"Oh please if that isn't the biggest crock of—"

"I'm going to Kingston to commit a crime."

Alice stared at Janet for close to a full minute.

"The less you know about it, the better it is for you. Say they arrest me. You can tell the police you have no idea what I was doing, and you'd be telling the truth."

"Does this have anything to do with Burt?"

Now it was Janet's turn to stare. "Why on God's green earth would it have anything to do with Burt?"

"I mean…I know he hurt you, but that was five years ago and there's no need to ruin your life for the sake of reven—"

"Wait a minute," said Janet. "Do you think I'm going to kill Burt?"

"Well, you said crime and Kingston and I thought—"

"Burt's in *Kingston*?"

"Jan…"

"How do you know where Burt is?"

"I have no fucking idea where Burt is. You said crime and you're borrowing black clothes, I thought murder, okay? End of story. And what do you think you're doing putting me on the defensive? I get in a car with you to go on your *Kingston crime spree*, no questions asked..."

"There were plenty of questions asked!"

"...and you've got the utter balls to put me on the defensive."

"You think I'd actually murder someone?"

"You said crime!"

"*There are other crimes besides murder!*" Janet breathed loudly through her nose, in and out, in and out, like someone who had just finished running a marathon. She noticed Alice was doing the same thing, and it occurred to her that, between the two of them, they might suck up all the oxygen in the car. Janet cracked a window and felt the thick summer air, cooled by the speed of her driving.

She wanted to hate Alice right now, hate her as if she'd forced her way into her car, as if she'd held Janet down and shoved her into her clothes. But all she could think of was what Alice had said to her, over the phone that night. *You sound upset. What can I do?* "All right you win!" Janet said, slapping the steering wheel so hard it made Alice yelp. "But don't say I didn't warn you..."

~

As Janet paid the toll clerk at the Kingston exit, Alice said, "Medical marijuana?"

"Ssssh."

"Honey, as far as misdemeanors go, buying doobie for a cancer patient—"

"Alice, the toll both operator."

"...ranks somewhere below jaywalking. The fact is, it's a *good* deed in this big, bitchy world."

Janet pulled away from the booth and headed into Kingston. "The fact is," she said through her teeth, "I'm going to be buying an illegal drug, putting it in my car with you and driving sixty miles with it in there. If a policeman pulls us over and finds it, I don't think telling him it's for a cancer patient is going to keep us out of jail in this big, bitchy world."

"Oh. I didn't think of it that way." Dark as it was in the car, Janet could tell Alice was blushing. For one racing moment, she looked exactly like Shane.

"Don't worry," said Janet. "We won't get pulled over."

They were entering what Janet figured was downtown Kingston. They passed a pawn shop and a Dunkin' Donuts and a coin laundry and a Chinese restaurant called Fong's with a big neon sign about the same age as Janet. The "n," the "g," the "'s" and half the "o" had burnt out, leaving "Fu" in pink cursive letters.

The restaurant was closed. Nearly every business was closed, except for Dunkin' Donuts. The street they were on was called Broadway. "The Lights of Broadway," Janet said, and laughed a little.

Alice didn't.

They passed a drive-through pharmacy and a Burger King and a One-Hour Photo and a beauty shop called Sultana that also did "body piercing and hair extensions." Janet imagined herself with hair down to her knees and a diamond stud in her belly button, just because it was something to think about. They passed a tattoo parlor called Phat Tats, and Janet imagined herself with "Steve Forever" scrawled across her backside.

They passed Kingston High School, an old, sooty building much larger than Leeds High. On the opposite side of the street was Kingston Hospital—large too, but younger, friendlier. Lights were trained on a banner, advertising the hospital's chronic pain unit in cheery orange letters: *When pain ends, life begins.*

"Steve Reynolds was gorgeous," said Alice.

"He still is."

"Really? Your mother said he looks like hell."

"How would my mother know what Steve looks like? She doesn't leave her house."

"True, but late-stage pancreatic cancer doesn't usually do much for the complexion."

Janet looked at Alice. "That's not very nice."

"It's just the truth, Jan."

"Well I've seen Steve, and you haven't, and he's gorgeous. As gorgeous as ever. More gorgeous, actually, because he's got character in his face."

"Okay, okay. Whatever."

Janet made a left turn at the Stewart's Shop, thinking, Whatever yourself Alice. You can just whatever yourself right out the window for all I care. Why did Alice have to use expressions like whatever, anyway? Did she think they made her sound young and with-it? Because they didn't. They made her sound middle-aged and silly. She might as well put on one of Shane's ridiculous T-shirts and go skateboarding in the Rec Center parking lot.

Alice said, "How come you two never kept in touch?"

"What do you mean?"

"Oh come, on. The little Italian restaurant in the Village with the guy with the violin? Champagne on the steps of St. Patrick's? And he kisses you and tells you he's wanted you forever? I mean, don't you think you'd at least get a postcard from him after a night like that?"

In her mind, Janet could see Steve's twenty-three-year-old face, leaning into hers. She could feel his hand against her back through the thin Mexican blouse; she could hear him whisper her name. As if it had just happened, Janet marveled at how his eyes glittered, at how he hadn't shut them to kiss her. "It was a perfect night," she said. "Lots of people live their whole lives without one."

"You always say that, but I don't think you'd be greedy to expect a fucking postcard afterwards."

Janet took a deep breath. Three counts in, three counts out. "You say it too much, you know."

"Pardon?"

"The f-word. You say it too much and it's unattractive."

"Oh give me a—"

"And you have no right to discuss Steve's condition with my mother. You don't even know him."

"What are you, the fucking *talking police*?"

"Shut up!"

Alice's eyes widened, but she did as she was told. They drove in silence past rows and rows of Victorian duplexes with empty porches and identical cropped lawns until they reached a brick building with The Haskell J. Weintraub Skilled Nursing Facility spelled across its façade in large metal letters. This was Israel's nursing home, which Alice knew because Janet had told her the name, but even then, her mouth stayed shut.

"I'm sorry. I'm just a little on-edge," Janet said as she pulled into the parking lot five minutes early, eyes peeled for Israel's "righteous, vintage pimpmobile" (Shane's words, not hers).

Finally, Alice spoke. "Please don't get us arrested, Janet."

~

The man who had to be Israel strode toward what had to be the pimpmobile—a lavender, late-seventies Cadillac with a vanity plate that said "EZRIDR."

He was handsome in a silly way, Janet thought. His hair had the type of sheen you'd associate with man-made substances—vinyl, for instance, or acrylic paint. His forearms bulged blatantly, his surgical scrubs were very tight, and matched the Cadillac. He must have been at least six-foot-seven.

– Prima Materia –

Peering into the women's car, he smiled. Around his neck, he wore a thick gold chain with a medallion in the shape of a cannabis leaf. "Good lord," said Janet, smiling back.

"That's the tallest Mexican guy I've ever seen," Alice said.

"You want me to go with you?"

"No, I'm fine." She meant it. There was something about the extremity of his height, his muscles, his chalk-white teeth, that put her at ease. It was as if she were buying drugs from an animated character.

As Janet got out of her car, she could have sworn she saw a tiny star, twinkling in one of his black eyes.

She led him out of Alice's hearing range. "Hi, I believe Shane spoke to you about me?" she said. "It's so nice of you to do this for me. I need it so badly. You take checks, don't you? By the way I just love your car it's so… unusual."

The man's smile loosened. "Who is Shane?"

~

After Janet got through explaining to the tall physical therapist—whose blue Hyundai was parked just to the left of the Cadillac—that she was not attempting to solicit sex from him, he directed her attention to Israel, a wan, balding man in his forties who had been sitting behind the wheel of his car all along.

The transaction was brief and perfunctory—not much different than buying stamps. Israel listened to Janet introduce herself and asked how much "product" she needed without even looking at her. How silly she'd been to worry about her clothes, to take her best friend along as protection, as if she were going on some sort of blind date. Yes, they were in the front seat of a pimpmobile in a parking lot at midnight, but for Israel, this was obviously just another day at the office.

The only time he looked at Janet's face was when she said, "I'll take one pound."

"That'll cost you $5,000."

"Shane said he charges $160 a half!"

"A half-ounce."

"Ounce?"

"We deal in ounces."

"But...this is for a cancer patient."

"We still deal in ounces."

So Janet bought an ounce, which Israel assured her was "a lot of product," even for a cancer patient. She left the Cadillac carrying a plastic sandwich bag full of bushy, pungent sprigs. It didn't look like a lot to her.

Before she got into the Cutlass, Janet held the bag out to Alice. "Does this look like a lot to you?"

"Put that *away*!"

"There's no one around."

"You've never heard of surveillance cameras?"

Janet shoved the bag in her purse, slid into the driver's seat and started up the car. "I should've gotten him to weigh it. Don't these people normally have scales?"

"How am I supposed to know?"

"I assumed..."

"You assumed wrong. I don't smoke pot, and I don't know anyone who does." Janet could smell the burning sweetness of the patchouli oil Alice daubed her temples with each day. In high school, she used to say the oil made boys consider her a "wild bohemian," and love her "relentlessly." Janet had met several of Alice's boyfriends over the years—including the Union College art student that went on to father Shane, marry another woman and move to Florida—and none of them had seemed particularly relentless. Yet Alice kept anointing herself with the stuff, every morning and every night. Did she still think it produced that effect in men? Did she still want it to, or was it just another habit—like coloring her hair—that made her feel like nothing had changed?

— Prima Materia —

It occurred to Janet that she and Alice didn't know each other anymore—at least, not the way they used to. As teenagers, they'd talk for hours about topics so intimate, they would have made Janet blush today: the feel of a boy's tongue in one's mouth; the potential ramifications of stuffing one's bra on prom night; the agonizing softness of Steve Reynolds' lips against the back of one's neck. "Alice," Janet said. "Are you dating anybody?"

"Why the fuck would you ask me that?"

"I was only making conversation."

"Oh, well I… It's just so late, and this is all so weird, and I guess I'm a little…"

"Scared?"

"There's a police car following us."

"He's just going in the same direction we are," Janet said. "It's okay."

She made a right turn when she saw the Lights of Broadway, and looked straight up at Kingston Hospital. She read the banner again, savored the words like orange candy.

When pain ends, life begins.

"I'm sleeping with Burt," said Alice.

Janet looked at her best friend of thirty-five years. She seemed to be examining her manicure.

"I wish I could think of a better way to tell you. I wish I didn't have to tell you at all, Honey. I know how much this must hurt. But…Burt and I are getting serious. We might even get married and…I just thought you should know."

"How much?" Janet said.

"Excuse me?"

"You said you know, so tell me. How much must this hurt?"

"Jan, I—"

"Whatever. Whatever, Alice. What-*fucking*-ever!" There was a lot more Janet wanted to say—*Get out of my car* being at the top of the list, but, as it turned out, she wasn't able to say any of it. The police car behind them was now flashing its lights, its siren bleating, warning her to pull over.

~

"License and registration," said the officer. No *Ma'am* afterward. No *Please*—just the necessary words. He was awfully young to be so stern, to be shining that flashlight into her eyes. His face was unlined; his cheeks even bore remnants of acne. Janet was certain everyone he ever loved was still alive.

"Would you mind telling me why?"

"Ssssh," said Alice.

"You didn't notice the stop sign back there? You drove right through it."

"Yes, well I guess there are a lot of things I don't notice."

The young officer raised his eyebrows.

"Jesus, Jan."

"I'm sorry," said Janet. "It's just...been a long day."

"License and registration." He shined the flashlight on Janet, then Alice, then Janet again. It made Janet feel like an unpleasant specimen, like a dead bug at a crime scene.

As she removed her wallet from her purse, Janet's hand brushed the freezer bag. Her heart sped up, but she made sure not to change her facial expression. Alice, meanwhile, was whispering, "Please, please, please...," her hands balled into desperate fists.

The officer retreated to his squad car to check Janet's record. "He probably saw us in the parking lot," said Alice. "I told you. How could you take that baggie out of your purse like that, in plain view of the entire—"

"We can't all be perfect, Alice."

– *Prima Materia* –

The two women glared at each other until the policeman returned.

"Can I ask you something, officer?" Janet said. "What would you say if you just found out your best friend was having an affair with someone who hurt you, terribly?"

Alice sunk very low in the car seat.

"I'd say…that's life," he said.

"That's life?" Janet said. "I don't happen to think that's life. I happen to think life should work out the way it's supposed to. I think people should get what they deserve, more or less. I happen to think life should be fair."

"Death's unfair," said the officer. "Getting sick's unfair. My grandma never hurt anybody but she's a diabetic and she lost her leg. That's unfair. You're probably a nice lady—look at the crappy car you drive. Life's full of unfair things."

"So why live at all?" Janet asked.

"I dunno… Chocolate-covered cheesecake?" He handed back Janet's license and registration, along with a $50 ticket. "Have a nice evening."

After the policeman drove away, Alice said, "Well that's a relief."

Janet didn't reply.

"You can hate me all you want. I deserve it."

Janet just sat there, staring at her hands, because it wasn't Alice she hated. The truth was, Burt *hadn't* hurt her terribly by leaving. She'd married him because he was quiet, and because he liked her cooking and, most of all, because it was something to do. But she hadn't thought of him in years—she barely remembered what he looked like. She didn't even care that Alice had been seeing him behind her back. Actually, it made her feel a little better about asking Shane for drugs.

No, it wasn't Alice she hated and it wasn't the $50 ticket and it wasn't even the fact that Steve Reynolds was dying, which he was, she knew. It was something else,

162

something harder to name. "I've never had chocolate-covered cheesecake," she said. And then she started to cry.

~

"Live a little," Steve Reynolds had said. "You'll never turn eighteen again."

Janet looked at his face in the reddish light of Rick's Ribs and then at Alice saying, "What are you waiting for?"

Then she looked across the bar, at all the cigarette tips glowing like city lights and the waitresses passing by with steaming plates of ribs, at all the men and women leaning into each other, shouting to be heard. So much fire around her, so much heat and hope and life.

"Let's go," she said. She followed Steve out onto the sidewalk, and he gave her the crook of his arm like an old-fashioned gentleman. Janet accepted it gracefully, she thought; Janet, who had never thought of herself as graceful. But there she was, on the arm of the star of so many of her fantasies, inhaling the summer air and feeling, not like herself at all, but like a leading lady, like Janet Leigh.

The red mustang had its top down, and Steve opened the door for her. After he got in beside her, she thought, *Mrs. Steven Reynolds, Janet Reynolds, Janet Clark Reynolds,* until she feared her heart might burst through her ribcage. "You ready?" he asked.

"No."

~

Janet laid her head on the steering wheel and sobbed. Powerful sobs that forced their way up her digestive tract, sobs that made her gasp and shake. She could feel Alice's hand on her shoulder, she could hear Alice's voice saying, "Oh God, Jan," again and again.

— *Prima Materia* —

Janet never cried. When her father died on the golf course of a massive stroke, Janet had said to Alice, "I'll cry about this later. There are funeral arrangements to be made." That was seven years ago and still Janet hadn't cried. When Burt had left her, she'd barely frowned.

But now, an hour past midnight in a parked car in front of Kingston Hospital, with a $50 ticket in her hand and an ounce of marijuana in her purse, Janet cried for Burt, she cried for her father, she cried for her Calphalon pot and her loneliness, and for that night—nearly thirty-two years ago to the day—when she'd asked Steve Reynolds to please drive her home, and left his car without kissing him goodnight.

Alice put both arms around her. Janet couldn't remember the last time she'd been hugged, and so she hugged her back, smelling the patchouli in her best friend's hair. She let Alice hold her, let her hand her Kleenex and stroke her hair and whisper "It's okay," like the mother she was, until her sobs subsided and she was left hoarse and hollow and calm.

~

When Steve had dropped Janet off, no lights were on at her parents' house.

"Gee," she said. "They usually wait up for me."

"You sure you don't want to come?"

Could she really feel the heat from his body when they sat at least a foot apart? Could she really feel the energy he expended, just by being alive and next to her? "I'd love to but…school starts in two weeks. There's so much stuff I have to do, and…"

"I'll get you back by noon. Promise."

"I've got to wake up early. My mother's taking me shopping. Maybe some other time."

"Headed back to Maui tomorrow night." He tapped the steering wheel with a tanned, strong hand and grinned. "And you're off to college."

Life is your movie, Cookie. You can make it into a comedy, or a romance, or a horror film, because you're the star and the director. Janet's mother had said that to her at graduation. Two whole months ago, but now it seemed like yesterday. Strange how memories worked, how they could flip back in front of you like a dog-eared page.

"Maybe I'll visit you in Hawaii some day," Janet said. "I mean, if I were to just show up on your doorstep, what would you do?"

"Teach you how to surf."

Janet got out of the car and said, "Maybe I'll do that, then."

"Great." Steve Reynolds' teeth were as white as his white T-shirt, and she knew she'd never see him again.

As she lay in bed that night, Janet didn't feel like a director or a star. She felt like an audience member—sitting alone in the dark, watching things happen without being able to change them, wanting her money back. She felt that way, all the way up until the following afternoon, when she called Alice and said, "Want to hear about my night in Manhattan with Steve?"

~

"Want to hear about my night in Manhattan with Steve?" Janet asked. Alice's shirt was wet with her tears, so she lifted her head from her shoulder.

"It was a perfect night," Alice said.

The truth is what you want it to be. Make us true, Janet, please... Had Steve actually said that to her on the car-ride home, or was it only something she'd told Alice he'd said? Looking at Alice now—looking into her eyes and seeing that strange emotion that had always been there when she talked about Steve, that hint of some unspoken thing she'd always assumed was jealousy—Janet understood it didn't matter. Alice knew the truth. She always had.

Janet said, "Lots of people live their whole lives without one perfect night."

"Tell me about the Italian restaurant again."

She started up the car and pulled away from the curb. "There were red candles on every table, but we were the only customers there."

"Oh, how romantic."

"There was this old, Italian man with a violin, and Steve asked him to play that song by Bread..." Janet glanced into the rearview mirror as she spoke. Through it, she could see Kingston Hospital, and its chronic pain unit, getting smaller and smaller, like a memory.

Families: Everybody Has One

Happiness is having a large, loving, caring, close-knit family in another city.

—George Burns

Flukenschweilers
Paloma J. R. Kopp
You sure made a lovely fire!
I made a lovely fire!
All right, son. I need to go on a business trip to New York city.
I made a lovely fire!
Now I need to go get ready.
I made a lovely fire...
Right now you can just enjoy your lovely fire.
I made a lovely fire
HEY! WHERE ARE ALL MY BOW TIES?!
I made—
They made a lovely fire!

Password

Sparrow

One day, when I was ten years old, my mother said to me, "I'm going out for a few minutes. The password is 'two-six-eagle.' If anyone says that, let them in the house."

I agreed. A few minutes later, I heard a knock at the door, and the words "two-six-eagle." I opened the door. An elderly man with a gray hat stood in the doorway.

"Come in," I said. He entered the house silently, and sat in a chair in the kitchen. There was a long pause.

"Do you have anything red to eat?" he asked finally.

I looked in the refrigerator. "How about a tomato?" I replied.

"Let me see it," the man ordered.

I showed him the tomato. He took it and ate it in three bites, dripping juice on the floor.

There was more silence. Then the man said, "Do you have a mirror?"

"Sure," I replied, rushing into my mother's bedroom. I returned with a small hand mirror. The man looked in it for a moment, then threw it on the floor.

Silence resumed. "May I have some salt?" the man inquired.

I brought him the saltshaker. He poured salt on his hand, and licked it off.

Shortly afterwards, my mother returned. When she saw the man, she smiled. "Jerry!" she said. She and the man kissed.

Moss

Lorna Smedman

The warm water felt cool against her hand compared to the sticky air, the way her face felt cooler when she tilted it up into the small puffs of wind her father created rowing the boat with easy steady strokes. As soon as she noted this, the sun beat through the top of their little shell of breeze as if it had read her mind and could not bear to be vanquished, even for a moment. "Hot?" asked her father, pausing to rest, his elbows wide on the upturned oars. There were large circles of damp under the arms of his thin green shirt. She vehemently shook her head no, plunging her hand deeper, wondering at the veins of golden light her fingers chased through the water. The boat glided forward a little, just a little, as her father unscrewed the thermos cap and poured out some iced tea, drinking half and then offering the rest to her. If she held her hand still, down under the surface where the water felt cooler, her skin was golden and rays of light shot out from the ends of her fingers. If she stretched her fingers wide, she could lengthen the rays like pulling on threads.

"Ready?" The girl sat up straight, wet hand on the edge of the boat, nodding, stashing the thermos under her seat this time. The man bit back a smile at her seriousness, furrowing his brows to match hers, then skimmed the oar shallow to splash her. "Don't," she cried sharply, and he did it again. An arc of wet dotted the front of her shirt. "Stop it." That sharpness in her voice piqued him. "It's just a little water." She hunched forward on the seat, grabbing her elbows, knees locked together, her face hard with anger. His own answering twinge

— Prima Materia —

of anger was buried under heavy bafflement. Where did his daughter's anger come from, welling up so big, so fast?

She was staring over his shoulder, as she had done steadfastly, but now she was silent, no longer carefully directing his rowing, this way, this way. And she was no longer looking at things, the light in the water or some slick green weeds flowing in the current near the bank or a sudden hollow thunk—things he had been watching her register with her various degrees of intensity, depths of intensity that almost frightened him. It was part of the reason he had kept on with these fishing trips with her. Sometimes he worried about the way she looked at things so hard.

She didn't even bother to smile when they passed under an overhanging willow and he yelped and shivered and flailed the oars in the water at the touch of the leaves on the back of his neck. She barely flinched as the supple branches struck fast against her face, just narrowed her eyes, making him feel stupid. She felt bad then, and wagging her wrist sang out, "Left, left..." He pulled the boat left, half glancing over a shoulder. "What..." "Only a log, Dad. Oh..." There was a small painted turtle sunning, and she swiveled to keep looking.

And then swiftly turned back, hunching over again with her arms awkwardly wrapped around her chest. The splashes had plastered the fabric of her shirt against the plump swell of her beginning breasts. He saw that, now. His daughter's hot embarrassment about her changing body, changes which startled him each time he noticed them, called out a sharp constriction inside his own chest. "It doesn't matter," he wanted to yell. It shouldn't matter. He was a stupid klutz.

She had kindness in her, he was glad of that. Quick to let him off the hook. It awed him a little. With her other wrist, she silently signaled right, an easy curve in the creek. "Gotcha boss," he said, not glancing back.

He had taken her fishing on a whim once last summer, setting her up with an old pole with a knotted-up reel. She watched him, and then threaded her own worm on the hook without much squeamishness. That surprised him. And when she hooked her first fish—a small bass that they ended up throwing back—she was so excited she couldn't stop talking about it. She would have eased the hook from the fish's mouth, too, if he had let her. So this year, for her twelfth birthday, at the beginning of the summer, he gave her a fishing pole, with a reel almost better than his own, and was gratified that she had been overwhelmed with surprise and delight. It wasn't often that he was able to surprise her anymore.

A fishing pole had been the last thing she expected from her father. She loved watching him fixing things, building a new set of stairs, a carport, putting in the patio. But he never let her touch any of his tools; in fact, she knew better than to even stand near his power saw or drill. When she was younger, he'd let her sort nails and screws and nuts, and she still did this for him, washing and saving peanut butter jars for that purpose. It wasn't that she was a tomboy. Far from it. Not interested in sports, or climbing trees. But getting up early, digging for worms, taking the boat out on the creek, and then rowing to her father's best fishing spots, the quiet, the mucky odor of the creek, wild masses of weeds tumbling over the banks, a thermos of iced tea between them—she loved this. She loved the tugging of a fish on her line, and admired her father's grace and skill in getting the fish to take his hook. Put yourself in the fish's place, he told her. Learn to think like it would think—that's how you outsmart them. When her line jerked and the bobbin disappeared, she was in two places at the same time: in the boat, never taking her eyes off the place where her line cut the water, and also under the water, skimming through the thick greeny-brown light, on the lookout for the right hole in the blurry tumble of rocks along the creek bottom.

She splayed the fingers of her right hand over the warm wood of the boat's edge, letting the sun bake her hand, noticing, between her fingers, how fast the water appeared to move. Looking out across the front of the boat, it seemed as if they were hardly moving at all. But if she just concentrated on the water she could see through the spokes of her fingers, they seemed to be going through the water fast. Looking up now, she cried out and urgently circled her hand to signal a sudden sharp curve. Her father quickly put up one oar and dug deep with the other. In the little space after the oar's splash they heard it, a panting keen, cut in half. Water sputtered against the back of the angled oar, and the boat smartly rounded the bend, the dry brush hanging off the bank scritching the aluminum.

Then all the flesh, a tangle of pale arms and legs on the bright overhang of moss, the smooth length of the boy on top of the still girl. One of her heels pressed into the curve of his calf, one of her hands molded the soft curve of his waist. They had turned their faces away. His arm, curled around her head, dented the golden fan of her hair spread out all across the greenness.

She didn't know why she knew but she knew they weren't dead, even though they didn't move at all. Later, remembering it, her face got hot because the desire—to reach out and let her hand trail over them as their boat floated past—was so strong it seemed as if she had actually done it. The warmth and coolness of their pale smooth skin under her fingers. They had been so close.

So close they almost fell into the damn boat, her father would think later on, nearly laughing at the picture. He'd heard them, had tried to check their forward motion, but it was too late. The creek took the boat around the sudden curve, he saw them, but more distinctly, saw them register in his daughter's eyes. A shock. Him, too, keeping the oars up so as not to make any noise. Tiptoeing by. Heaped clothing, jeans, briefs, a pink bra. There had been sleek fine light hair along the girl's thigh, glinting in the sun. Every time he thought about the difference the presence of his daughter in the boat made, it was like the back of his stomach getting punched. Goddammit, who would have guessed? He had finally pulled away from there as hard as he could, his daughter's eyes focused over his shoulder, everything on the bank motionless until the boat began rounding the next bend, then quick pink leaping, nipples. There was nothing he could have done, even if he had heard them earlier, but that didn't help. He wanted nothing more than to get the damn boat out of the water, walk back and get the car.

"Aren't we going to fish?" she finally asked, her voice shaky. She had been watching her father's face, sometimes panicked, sometimes angry. He was navigating the boat himself now, as if she no longer existed, frequently looking over his shoulder, rowing hard and steady. They passed their best fishing spots, the deep spot in the shade of some trees behind the giant fallen trunk, its roots reaching out of the water like witches' fingers, the place near the big rocks. He rested a moment, his elbows angled out balancing the oars. "I think we better just go back now." She looked away, her eyes filling. "Why?" It came out whiny, like she was seven or eight years old again.

He put up the oars, and leaned forward with his elbows on his knees, his head down, slowly combing his fingers through his hair. She twisted in her seat, slipping her hand down in the water, pressing her stomach hard against the side of the boat to keep from crying. Golden threads shot out of the ends of her fingers, then retracted and disappeared as she clenched her hand.

"They had no goddamn business being there, those kids," he finally said, still looking at the bottom of the boat. He was trying to sound mad, but he wasn't. "I know," she answered, too quickly. If she tilted her hand, and zigzagged her fingers, the lines criss-crossed and got bent down. She plunged in her other hand, weaving a kind of glinting web with the light from all ten fingertips. The sharp rap of metal against metal made her jerk her eyes up. Her father, standing, swung the coffee can in an arc, flinging the loosened dirt and worms out over the water. "Christmas in July," he said, grinning at her. The outrage of it made her feel like she would never smile again. Instead she went down in the water, down alongside the worms thrashing in their dirty milky cloud, then down further until she was inside the rocks, looking up from that good hiding place at the worms steadily drifting down and the bulky silvery bottom of the boat breaking the green-gold shining surface of the water.

Three Poems

Celia Bland

The Brain Tree

My mother didn't shave
under her arms. Hanging clothes on the line
I glimpsed blackberry brambles in her dark pits.

My stepfather believed
women should not shave, wear panties, or eat canned soup.
No deodorants, no aluminum foil.
We washed our clothes in cold water.
Some things never came out.

His dislike embarrassed me.
I walked like a dinosaur, chewed rocks,
never helped. In the bathroom
he cut newspaper into neat squares.
When these were dirtied,
he burned them.

Taking in the clothes, I stepped
on a rusty nail left from his cold frame.
Unfinished its plastic roof
snapped in the wind.
Ice sheathed the tomato plants and green
drained from their spatulate leaves.
In spring, only the skins were left, stinky and seedy.
he jerked out their dead roots.
We were moving anyway.

— *Prima Materia* —

Tomato pulp reminds me of him.
On an airplane, I pierced my cherry tomato
and it exploded onto the coat of the woman beside me.
A little brain.
She said, "This will never come out!"
Out the window, North Carolina
was a leathery skin.
My shadow moved over the land
darkening houses and plowed fields.
My brain was blossoming
atop its stem: the medulla oblongata,
the cerebellum, pulsing and pocked.
I landed at La Guardia knowing no one –
just what I could say
and what would never come out.

— *Celia Bland* —

Permanent Record

The time
Principal Gerringer
slapped my fanny
I was lying
for my mother's
amusement.
She was not
amused.
She called him
yowling like a mother
cat.
I *had* been slapped
but the principal
was Sister Salome
and it was second grade
not fifth
and in another state
in a Catholic school.
I'd never told
that time.
Principal Gerringer
protested his innocence but she
believed me.
I decided to put the whole thing
behind me
but the principal
pulled me
from assembly
guiding me with his hand
from the line
to look in my face.
"I'm sorry,"
he said.

Jaundice

Still bleeding from your birth
I watched you ripen in silence.
In two days, your scrotum was a perfect apricot.

You slept as I ran to the clinic, the lab,
the emergency room, releasing you
to a Plexiglas incubator,
a specialist, a plethora of residents. Still, I bled
as I gave you up for dead.

But when they pierced
the backs of your hands,
irrigating my blood
from the fine-strings they called veins,
you opened your yellow eyes and screamed.
Milk spurted from my breasts.

I would not let you go hungry into a strange soil.

From Travels with My Aunt

Rachel X. Weissman

1.

I'm six and have awoken in the middle of the night to discover I'm blind. Instead of my eyes slowly adjusting to my darkened bedroom, I see only black. I wait. Nothing. No bureau, no teddy bear, no doorway. My whimper escalates to a scream. Hours seem to pass, and then I hear the heavy thud of my father's bare feet on the parquet floors of our Upper West Side apartment.

"What's going on here?" he asks gruffly.

Between sobs, I manage to sputter out, "I'm blind, I can't see..."

"Wait a minute," he says and thuds out of the room.

Water runs in the bathroom for a minute and then thud thud thud he's sitting beside me on my twin bed littered with the twenty-some-odd stuffed animals I sleep with every night.

"Keep still a moment," he says, his hand holding my chin up. I brace myself, but already feel relieved.

Relieved because with my sleep-smelling father beside me in his cotton pajamas with the white piping, nothing could really be that bad. Then a warm wet sensation on my face, on my eyes, as the washcloth gently rubs the sleep crud from my lids until one eye opens and blackness fades to gray, the familiar outline of my father appearing. Light smears across my window shades as the tires of cars moving north and south on West End Avenue hiss on wet cobblestones. The features of his face come into focus and I see that he's very tired.

"Come on, let's get back to sleep."

He lies down beside me, wrapping an arm around my shoulder. I remember the sound of his breath, the musty chemical smell he brought with him from his darkroom, and the blanket of total safety I felt that night, my father having shown me he could vanquish blindness itself.

2.

My mother's poaching eggs. She yelps when the yokes break and uses a small egg poacher contraption made of aluminum. I've told her a million times that aluminum causes early senility. My father and I are sitting next to each other at the Formica slab extending from the wall that is our kitchen table. We're talking about Marsden Hartley, the British painter who grabs you by the guts when he's not painting British flags.

"Marsden who?" my mother asks.

"Marsden Hartley," I say.

"Oh," she says and continues minding her eggs.

"I love his deep purples and pinks," I say. "They massage my eyes."

"Oh sweetheart, you really know how to look at a painting. That's from my side of the family," says my father, beaming at me. He's elated that the years of dragging me through museums have finally paid off.

"Heartfull. I don't think I've heard of him," muses my mom, jiggling the insert in the aluminum poacher that causes early senility.

"It's Hartley, though he is really heart felt," I say.

My dad and I are beaming our heads off. The room is setting, the walls are bathed in pink and purple and the ceiling is rising.

"Honey, would you watch the clock and count thirty seconds when I say 'go'?"

"Sure, Mom."

She's mesmerized by the water, hands held pensively at her sides.

"Go!" As the second hand chugs around the face of the blue enamel clock my dad begins whistling "As Time Goes By." I chuckle. What a card.

3.

Standing in front of the bathroom mirror in a Best Western hotel in Pikesville, Maryland. Just out of the shower where I'd started scrubbing myself beneath hot jets of water. Under my nails, grayish oily skin-dirt appears as red marks do on my chest and neck. I'm 14. Cousin Marsha with the unfortunate black hairy arms is getting married and my parents are on the verge of divorce. My father has taken this opportunity to share the reason: Like Jan Morris, whose story I read in the New York Times magazine a few months ago, my father tells me that he too is a woman trapped in a man's body. I lift my chin and continue scraping along my neck. The stuff gathering beneath my nails is darker and the scraping never reaches the bottom, the actual pure skin, clean and free of dirt. He will never undergo the operation known as sex reassignment surgery, he assures me. Living in a man's body is the penance he'll pay to continue being my father.

Back in the city after the wedding I am agitated, panicked, but a bit euphoric, teetering on the edge of a strange abyss. I consult Patti, the sexy live-in babysitter of a friend's little sister, who has been tutoring us in the art of seduction nigh on a year, using a peeled banana to demonstrate technique. She tells me that we are all male and female and that my father is just a more extreme example.

4.

Late afternoon summer light dapples the trailer floor like beads of butter seeping into a warm piece of toast. My arm is wrapped around Robert's chest and I take a deep breath. At last I've reached an equilibrium: my lover and me in our weekend trailer home set thirty yards from my father's Catskill cabin. We've formed a strange trilogy of souls whose easy rapport is full of fart jokes and late-night discussions on the merits of Liz Taylor's black slip in *Butterfield 8*. It has allowed me to cease hating the parent whose fateful choice has colored almost everything in my life since adolescence.

Robert stirs and turns, kisses my forehead sleepily and then goes back under.

I wake and it's dark out, but the light above the bed is blinking on and off.

"Robert, dinner's ready," I whisper. My father is signaling us by jiggling the extension cord that supplies juice to the trailer.

Julia Childs has aided him in the preparation of a roast leg of lamb appointed with fresh sprigs of rosemary—a meal that took him hours to prepare, but which is par for the course now that he's made cooking his passion. He bustles cheerily in the kitchen, an apron stretched over his surgically improved bosom. It will always be irksome to hug him—I don't want to encounter those too large, too strangely shaped, too projectile-like objects that really don't belong on my handsome father, objects that have in fact changed him into some other. At least here, safe from the scrutiny of sophisticated New York City eyes, he has stopped wearing tweed suits that June Cleaver might don—my father's idea of femininity so bizarrely retro—and he has ceased to whisper, forgoing the effort to mask the deep voice that fifty years of testosterone won't allow to lighten. At least I can hear my father's voice again, his laugh too, laughter at his own corny depression-era humor: "Mom,

Mom, how long till we reach Miami?" "Shut up, kid, and keep swimming." Besides my father there is Chiclets, the small white dog whose fur is one great dreadlock and to whom my father throws bones from the supper table. Bones that we never find again, because she eats them in their entirety.

5.

Bad day. Pop blew up at the woman at the health food store who helped me pick out the correct herbs and dietary supplements that might reverse the cancer that has already spread from his lungs to his spine. The acupuncturist has refused to see him after a last minute cancellation. He won't eat the strawberry ice cream I've churned for him in the ice cream maker I spent too much money on; he won't eat the hamburger I've fried him; he won't eat anything, in fact, and refuses to wear the size five Hanes Her Way underwear I bought him at the Kingston Super K-Mart, correctly believing that a 5'11" man/woman needs a larger size, but not realizing that one who has shrunk from 175 to 110 pounds in fact should wear a size five. His metabolic rate has risen, causing him to overheat constantly. He strips off his clothes even when modest guests come to visit, and the elastic of the leg holes lays flaccid on his thighs, the too-large underwear slipping to reveal the surgically-created vagina that I've fought for so many years not to see.

I rent *Smoke*, a movie I think will comfort, based on Paul Auster stories, starring a sweet Harvey Keitel. My father is anxious and keeps commenting on how depressing the innocent movie is. He wants to get out, to drive. Anywhere. We prepare to leave, but then he decides it won't help.

"You look tired," he says.

"Yes, here, I'll leave Chiclets with you," I say, dumping the warm creature from my lap and preparing to make my way to the trailer below.

"No, take her. I think you need her more than I do."

I kiss him goodnight and carry her down the dark driveway and across the patch of moss to my bed in the trailer.

Discovering that the half-wild dog loves to be held like a stuffed animal—a dog who until now has slept beneath my father's desk amid dust balls and electrical cords—has been the best antidote to the hopeless situation I find myself in during these last days.

Once in bed, I hold her and weep into her soft fur. I weep for the untouched meals and for my father's shrinking form—a form that has betrayed me more than once. As my tears wane, I see through the window facing the cabin a light sweeping back and forth as it approaches the trailer. A loud knock on the aluminum storm door, and he enters.

Standing in the doorway, emaciated, but with a look of concern on his face that I can't remember having seen for months, he hands me the flashlight.

"Here, take this. I don't want you to be frightened in the dark," he says.

And leaves.

Observations.
ଔ Asides. ଓ
Epiphanies.

There's One!

Mary Leonard

My mother-in-law visits from Iowa. She's eighty-seven and in good physical health. The social worker at her senior residence tells us, "She doesn't need any medications." On the first hour of her visit, she moves all the wicker furniture on our front porch and sweeps. The porch looks perfect when I return home from work.

 I pick up my mother who also lives in a senior residence. She is eighty-six, blind in one eye, deaf in one ear (luckily not on the same side), recovering from a major heart attack, and walking off balance. She relaxes in the wicker rocker and Shirley, my mother-in-law, starts lamenting about her memory loss. "My mind is going. I can't remember anything anymore. I'm so confused. My mind is going. Sometimes I don't have any memory." My mother, who only hears what she wants to hear, hears only the word, "memory."

 "Memories are wonderful things. We should never lose hold of our memories. It's all we have now. I close my eyes and remember all the good times. At least I have my memories. My mind is still good."

 I stand up and scream, "Haven't you two been listening to each other?"

 They look at me with disbelief. My mother says, "We're having a nice conversation. Why are you yelling?"

 It's early in the week of Shirley's visit and I haven't abandoned my middle-aged pragmatism. Once I accept that I have a minor role in the theater of the absurd, I plan my moves accordingly.

 "I'm taking the mothers out to lunch at the diner, "I tell my husband. He's very grateful because it's so difficult to have a conversation with someone who is so disoriented, and he realizes that his mother's visit to Kingston was a mistake, that we must visit her where she is more secure. At our house, Shirley spends her days rearranging her possessions so that she can find what she hasn't lost. Sometimes she hides things so that we won't take them and then we all spend the day in a scavenger hunt.

I have decided that the diner would be the easiest, the most generic and familiar restaurant, forgetting that the menu has hundreds of choices. Shirley and I help my mother up the stairs and we all study the menu until my mother says, "Order for me. You know what I like and anyway I can't see the menu." I look at the menu, scanning for what she might enjoy. "They have veal Marsala, Mom." She says, "Fine." That was easy, I think, too easy.

Shirley is still looking at the menu, and then says, "Chicken, what's that?" I panic. The menu is eight pages long and what if I have to explain every meat, drawing pictures and making barnyard sounds. I am also saddened, realizing how far Shirley's mind has deteriorated if the word "chicken" doesn't register. That must mean that she has lost her memory of her own roast chicken, chicken soup, and her famous chicken salad made with almonds. I reach down to some primal level and ask, "How about some spaghetti and meatballs?" Shirley is enthusiastic, recalling some memory of this dish she never cooked.

The food arrives and when my mother sees my pita bread sandwich, she wants it. So we switch. Shirley sees the mound of spaghetti and meatballs and says, "I can't eat all of this!"

"We'll take it home," I say and those two lines become the litany for the meal: "I can't eat all of this. We'll take it home." Meanwhile my mother has withdrawn into memories of better times. I talk rapid-speed about the children, their grandchildren, and Shirley says, "There's another one." While I have been talking, she's been noticing cars on the road next to the diner. "Another one" refers to red cars only, seemingly her favorite. My mother can't see that far and so she says, "Yes, there are too many flies in this diner."

I pay the bill and wonder if it's better to have a sound mind or a sound body. Just at the stage in my life when I have accepted the mind/body connection, I am contemplating the mind/body separation. On the way home, Shirley says, "It's a great life if you don't weaken." I point to a red car and say, "There's one!"

Seitan's Minion

Richard Klin

> An unfamiliar love welled up...for all that crawls and flies, breeds and swarms.... The Messiah Himself could not redeem the world as long as injustice was done to beasts.
> —Isaac Bashevis Singer, "The Slaughterer"

To be perfectly blunt, he had always looked with slight contempt at those who abstained from meat.

The contempt was rooted in misconceptions and stereotypes of a distinctly mid-seventies tenor: a harsh regimen of self-denial and priggish adherence to inedible food, a didactic, decaffeinated milieu of over-earnest folk music and wheat-grass juice. And the broader concept of animal rights—with which he vaguely sympathized—seemed very well-intentioned but just a little...irrelevant; subordinate to greater, meatier causes.

Early on, though, he had made an exception for veal—hardly a staple in his diet—the blatant cruelty involved in its processing so extraordinarily cruel that abstaining seemed hardly a sacrifice. The first real shift, though, had been in renouncing duck. On regular strolls through Brooklyn's Prospect Park he had become acquainted with the local duck colony, a species he soon came to greatly admire: their intrinsic dignity in the face of a somewhat silly waddle and widespread derision of the word *quack*, their pluckiness and industry.

When he first met her, the woman who was to become his wife, many of his misguided vegetarian misconceptions were immediately dispelled. She was a vegetarian of twenty years' standing, a strict consumer of organic products, a fervent believer in animal rights—and completely non-didactic, not in the least bit preachy, and just as interested in Dick Van Dyke reruns as he was.

A meat-free household seemed like an acceptable compromise, akin to keeping a kosher home for your spouse's sake. And of course, there was nothing to stop him from ordering meat outside the house.

The shift was gradual and had no specific point of origin. Certainly much was owed to his wife. Her low-key, easygoing vegetarianism gave him the mental space to let certain concepts shift around and gradually assume form. Her cooking was shockingly good too—it appeared that vegetarian cuisine had made huge strides since the era of Earth Day, and could hardly be considered self-denial. And their recent move from New York City to the rural Hudson Valley was another sea-change: a few miles from their new home was a cattle farm—freezer orders a specialty—and he would pass by almost every day.

And there it was, undeniably: mothers with their young, hanging out, nuzzling, grazing, spending time together. And more uncomfortable thoughts edged their way in. Practically his entire family had died in the Holocaust. He had long taken great offense to the spate of gratuitous Holocaust metaphors, the all-too-ready invoking of the death of the six million. The Holocaust, everybody's favorite hobbyhorse.

But now there seemed to be a comparison that really didn't seem so far-fetched. Here was a community of creatures, confined, imprisoned, living out their captive days until killing time. And this little cattle farm, he knew, was mild compared to larger, uglier enterprises. But it became increasingly uncomfortable to drive by day after day.

And there was more. The hitherto-parochial cause of animal rights suddenly did seem in fact linked to the greater global struggle. There was nothing quite as reprehensible as the meat industry and the crushing, ubiquitous fast-food empires—so responsible for the gutting of sustainable development, exploitative of land and labor; union-busting and predatory.

So he gave up meat and initially it really was wrenching. The shock to his system necessitated eating peanut butter straight from the jar, uncomfortably hearkening back to his teenage years—minus the convenient excuse of substance abuse. It seemed unthinkable that he would never eat rare roast beef again. Instead of fantasizing about fame or wealth, his thoughts dwelled on the bacon he had often enjoyed at the Acropolis Diner.

For over a year now he has lived meat-free. The earlier cravings have largely disappeared. The past Thanksgiving was celebrated in a turkeyless state, something of a watershed, and so was the polite renunciation of his 93-year-old grandmother's chicken soup with rice. There are still times when he feels paroxysms of meat longing. A commercial can set him off, or the smell of barbecue.

He wonders how he can tell this story without sounding like a self-righteous new convert. He is not in the least inclined to preach to anybody, knowing all too well what a commitment it is to purge one's diet of meat, how difficult it is to alter long-established patterns of eating, how personal the decision is. He joined PETA and reads their dispatches with horror. Animals are so innocent; so innocent and so totally without guile, so trusting and so utterly, utterly dependent, and so utterly without protection. There's not much that can be done about the loss of his family in the camps. He can't bring back his grandmother from Auschwitz. All he can do is not consume living creatures, which may not be much, but seems appropriate.

When you've made a contract with yourself that these are living, thinking creatures, there's really no going back. He hopes some day to adopt a duck and is phasing out all his leatherwear. To offset any potential hyperbole or bathos, he tried to give his essay a snappy, irreverent title. He has no neat, inspiring wrap-up. Do no harm, he thinks.

Stupidity Wins

Carl Frankel

Yesterday Mitchell told about a neighbor. Eight acres clearcut, the good aged wood burned, a wetland destroyed, all those helpless permits flouted, the property thrown on the market soon after for a quick buck.

Listening, I thought— *'How relentlessly the world spits up stories like this!'* I thought of all the forests ravaged, and the rivers poisoned, and all the rapes and murders everywhere, everyday, of every sort, and I thought, *'Oaf by oaf, we are destroying the world. What sort of justice, what sort of Law, is this?'*

And then I heard, or thought I heard, a voice, or maybe it was thunder: "**RESISTANCE IS FUTILE. STUPIDITY ALWAYS WINS.**"

Today these thoughts are still with me and I ask: *'Who wrote this Law? What sort of god, or godlessness, would play this cheap, cruel trick? Is there an Author, or is this just a tacky tale starring Blind, Dumb, Stupid Evolution?'* Either way, my question is the same: *'STUPIDITY ALWAYS WINS—what sort of law is this?'*

Oh, I know what you'll say in your silky voice. One word: "**SURRENDER.**" Oh yes, I know your serpent ways. And yet I will defy you and say: *'I should love... this? I should have faith in... this?'*

And yet I persist, and I persist, and I persist, insisting on the right to a world where Stupidity is not the Law but the occasional aberration—and what sort of grand, quixotic Stupidity is this? Is it not monumentally Stupid of me to believe in the genius of Justice? And yet I persevere, and persevere, repeating to myself, as if in prayer, words that came to me once, as if whispered from the Abyss: *'Persist, persist. Yes, be that Stupid! Is any bet better? Fight on, fight on. Remember the law:* ***STUPIDITY ALWAYS WINS.****'*

Fourth of July

Guy Reed

I awoke this patriotic morning from a strange dream in which I was living on the West Bank with a radical Palestinian group, all of us hiding out in a decaying apartment building. I was working undercover, but undercover for whom or what I didn't know. It felt dangerous. There were two other undercover agents and one of them was discovered. After that, my cover was blown in association. I expected to be executed. However, I began to wash the dishes and spoke about my beliefs and non-beliefs in God, which won the favor of the leader of the group. Several men then interrupted us, bursting through the door in anger at me because I missed a wedding where I was to be the only "white guy." Suddenly, following the angry men, a spry-looking Bob Hope came through the door of the apartment. I was surprised to see him even in my dream mind, but it must have broken the mood in the apartment. I was no longer the only white guy in the place. I kept thinking about telling everyone back home of my travel adventure. "How shallow," I thought. I also wondered how my intense, hot-zone and subsequent narrow escape experience would change my life. As the dream faded to waking consciousness I saw brightly-colored plastic bits like the tips of neon red, white, and blue plastic forks broken off and stuck with the food in the drain-catch when I finished the dishes. Awake, I felt odd at hearing myself talk about God and discovering a lot of my feelings on the spot. I never declared a name to my belief because for me God is somewhere between *Seth Speaks*, Crazy Horse, metaphysics, quantum mechanics, mushrooms, birds, elephants, whales, the dream realm, irises in bloom, Van Gogh, Cezanne, and Rodin, the *Tao Te Ching*, reincarnation, synchronicity, the South Dakota prairie, poetry,

– Prima Materia –

photons, Bach, Beethoven, and Buddha, the Dalai Lama, Jimi Hendrix, Johnny Cash, P.J. Harvey, grapes, pears, bleu cheese, bread, and brie, a child's wide-eyed joy, the *Duino Elegies*, any prose written by Annie Dillard, a Raymond Carver poem, a breeze on the beach off the breaking Pacific, *Wings of Desire*, *Grand Illusion*, *Chinatown*, *Koyaanisqatsi*, and *Amelie*, the lavender and green in the twilight and dawn, fresh running water, a homerun in the bottom of the last inning, hope, humor, grace, chocolate cake, and ice-cold milk. That's the short list and still the spirit weaves through everything. Anyway, I saved my life by humbly washing the dishes of the Palestinians and sharing the simple wonderment in the mystery of the Great Spirit, the mystery of God. Religious freedom, wasn't that the agreement in the first place?

Guilt...
   Obsession...
       Mercy...

Bluebeard

Duff Allen

Deeply annoyed, whenever I looked, and, wherever I had looked, no matter where I looked, I continued to look and, even in my memory, I could not find Max Frisch's fabulous book, *Bluebeard*. Something distinct but not named told me that I had been carrying the magnificent murder book in my sack, which no matter where I go and no matter what I do, I carry hanging from my shoulder on a strap. This time I had signed it out from the local library, not to read it myself, as over the years I have read and reread it many times myself, reading it in the middle of the night and laughing at its murderous state of mind, but to give it away; not forever, since I did not own the book, but to give it away on loan from the local library for the pleasure of my knowing that there was a woman I knew reading Max Frisch's diabolical and very brilliant book, *Bluebeard*.

I had purposefully gone to the local library, to the exact spot at the end of the aisle near the wall between the wooden cases holding up hundreds and hundreds of unreadable modern books, mostly unreadable American books, if the truth be told, to pull out of rows of unreadable books the one readable book not for me to reread again, as I have done over the years to amaze myself with Max Frisch's clear and funny mind at work, but to have this book, along with others which I happened to be reading or thinking of reading myself at the time, in my sack to give to a woman with whom I had been sleeping and in some way I wanted to get back at by passing off to her Max Frisch's *Bluebeard* to read when, by chance, I should pass her in the street. Naturally, I would pass her by chance so it would never be known that for close to two months I had already been carrying Max Frisch's *Bluebeard* in my sack, which, when I met her would look like a kindly made and somewhat capricious suggestion when I pulled the thin well-translated volume out of my sack hanging as always from my shoulder. I was waiting for the day that, driven nearly mad by the mindcast of the woman whom I meant to insult by loaning to her the local library's volume of Max Frisch's *Bluebeard*, I was able to haphazardly bump into her and just as haphazardly, so it appeared, have with me the copy of *Bluebeard* which, out of my capricious generosity and interest in this woman, whose face I cannot remember, I had meant to believe I was loaning the local library's excellent translation of the Swiss writer's book *Bluebeard*.

Since my library privileges have been for some time, on account of Max Frisch's book, *Bluebeard*, not being returned, suspended, I am suspicious of a certain unnamed woman. After I called her exactly thirteen months from the date Max Frisch's great book was checked out, at which point of time I had lost all privileges to take any books, magazines, or compositions away from the library until *Bluebeard* were finally after so many threatening notices returned to it or paid for in full, more than a year after someone did not bring *Bluebeard* back to the library, she returned my call immediately that day denying knowing of or ever even hearing of this book, which, I believe, is a lie, since all I talk about with women is Max Frisch's book, *Bluebeard*, virtually all the time with virtually all the women I sleep with to get a sense of their intelligence and general sense of humor. While this unnamed and essentially non-intellectual woman may not be the one, with whom I did continue to have sex for matters of sexual continuity, although I do not think very highly of her, along with my having sex on and off with a continuous number of other more or less interesting women off and on over the same span of time, if it is not she who is, in truth, lying to me about Max Frisch's book, *Bluebeard*, then any number of other women are also lying to me.

    At one time I was able to quote passages from Max Frisch's book, *Bluebeard*, and, to my amusement did so frequently in bed at any time that one of the passages I had memorized floated upwards to my head; which, like the trick of any new music I heard effortlessly reproduced on a piano if I heard it once, should the text of *Bluebeard* have come to mind, I reproduced pages and pages of it for any of the women I was having sex with at the time. For some reason, in some way, I have always been more interested in reproducing music and passages of literature than I have been with women themselves, numbers of which I can no longer recall.

    Whenever I used to look at a score, the way a smiling woman smelling a rose brings happiness, I used to be able to hear everything. Though I am not permitted to remove any musical scores or any other books from the premises of the local library, I am permitted to go upstairs where for hours I examine the full symphonic scores of the great composers whose art I used to be able to hear playing in my head. Now, I look at the yellow symphonic music and feel myself straying between terror and grief. For hours, when I witness myself, sitting upstairs examining the masters' symphonic texts I feel my body's gravity turning to either side of terror or grief. Looking at the symphonic arrangements, which once a garden of musical joy they were to me, now, moving my finger vertically down a page, the simultaneous scores of different orchestral instruments whose time is written out, I move my finger so, horizontally across the page, now this means nothing more than something between terror and grief to me. Not able to put my finger on it now exactly, it makes my uneasy about everything.

What means almost nothing once almost meant everything. What I once enjoyed without effort I now no longer sense at all. Likewise, today, when the days pass, when I call no women and no women call me, when each year I pull out the tack and throw the calendar in trash, and, through the clean perforation at the top of the next calendar's top page, push the tack through it and back into the wall's tiny hole, even when I masturbate I cannot remember the names of any women, I cannot remember their faces, I cannot remember any of them.

Someone stole Max Frisch, and I do not know who it is.

For ages this thought troubled and bothered me. Until I had forgotten all women, all music, until I gave up worrying that, having forgotten them all, I was doomed, I was doomed. It is possible, I said, to myself recently, biting the end of my pencil with my teeth to sharpen it, too lazy to get up and get a kitchen knife to do the job, that I lost Max Frisch! Even if I did not lose Max Frisch, I need only pretend, I thought scribbling some of these notes to myself down, and others not, that it was not they but I who has lost that infamously famous foreign book!

I lost Max Frisch. It is I who lost Max Frisch's book, the lovely hardbound edition of *Bluebeard* belonging to the local library which I do not remember doing but will one day, I think, replace.

Three Poems

Nancy Rullo

Welcoming Alfred and Mervin
Jewish Refugees – 1949

In my gloves as white as ash I stepped with Alfred
around the ballroom dancing class.
My sister swung his brother and they laughed

at their tripping, those young ones. They
watched me dancing with Alfred, our care-filled steps
measured, nothing wasted. One, two, three;

one, two, three. Alfred's feet met mine as if
running in the wrong direction, dragging Mervin,
learning to count in each burning country,

in new silent languages, counting to three:
ready, set, go. We barely knew these boys
from the new synagogue on Clinton Avenue

but Alfred and I danced, each step as the teacher
commanded, meticulous nine-year-olds, fearful
of the frivolity of Mervin and Mary Alice

flying into the waltz as if they could light a fire
across the world, as if they didn't know
what all that smoke could mean.

– *Nancy Rullo* –

A Near Occasion of Sin

When I was a child I believed
I did not belong on Long Island.
I lay coiled under the apple tree
with a book, yearning for Russia.

When I was a child I believed in
exemplary behavior
sidestepping movies
offensive to The League of Decency,
watching for fork-tongued serpents.

Several snakes lived under the chicken coop
but the hens were long gone,
the victory garden all weeds.
My father was dead.
I hadn't been able to prevent that
no matter how many prayers
I hissed toward heaven.

I learned to watch my tongue
for its surprising
and delicious venom
and was lured by dreams
of hair in thick Russian braids,
a collar tall and starched–
Still life of a princess.

When I was a child I read too much, they said,
but I broke the lock
to the glass-covered book shelf.
My mother held the key.
My father was dead.
Tolstoy was forbidden.

– Prima Materia –

That Karenina woman,
a serpent in her husband's life,
was a near occasion of sin in mine.

Each day, all summer,
the McCarthy hearings rattled on TV,
my aunts tempted my mother
with spoonsful of blackberry brandy
for her nerves, checked me daily
for deviations, loose tongue and excessive literature,
then went home to read The Cardinal
in installments clipped monthly from Redbook.

At night I read by flashlight.
In my dreams I went as far as I could:
home to Russia, where my father
might be emperor. It snowed all the time.
It was too cold for snakes.

I didn't tell anyone how
I edged my back against America,
rubbing myself with my dreams,
dragging the length of my betrayal
through the now unfertile garden,
as if I could slough that poisoned year
and shed my skin, thick
with lies and secret textures.

I still read too much. But I've stopped
watching my tongue. Now it forks and flickers where it will.
I am no longer afraid of losing Paradise.
I have grown used to the taste of banishment.

– Nancy Rullo –

Indulgences

49th Winter Afternoon
without a True Blue
* Cigarette by My Side*

I planned to write a poem today except, well,
I am wrapped in a blanket unable to
imagine what meaning means or how to wres-
tle with the words it needs, so when you went
to buy new fencing in Kingston, the door
closed behind you like a slap of loneliness
on my cheek. (The meaning of lonely? who knows?
Like beauty, you know it when it appears.) When
you left I thought I'd write some, but chose to
indulge instead, eat dark chocolate. I wanted
to die, really die, but I lit candles (tea

lights that die themselves when the wax has burned – so
the house will not go up in smoke if I am
gone or gone crazy or if the flame goes crazy)
and burn musky incense as if this deepening
afternoon were a tryst with myself
 I would be dressed in a black lace slutty gown...
   I keep myself above the loneliness that...
   I want to sleep for... I curl on the couch that...
On TV even John Wayne looks good. He is
young, named Ringo the Kid, riding on a stagecoach with Dallas the whore; Mr. Peacock the

wimpy whiskey salesman; a soldier's wife, pale,
blond, heading for the fort; a gambler who shoots

– *Prima Materia* –

his enemies in the back; and a doctor,
called Doc, a drunk of course, whose salvation rides
on whom he will save in the movie, but as
he drinks his way through the first half hour, I have
a vodka, joining the doc in his lonely...
This you should know is against all the rules I
have set for my life – Thou shalt not kill, thine own-
self especially, and never drink before
sundown unless it is summer at the beach

where mimosas are not only beautiful,
but fitting at noon, when the ferry calls from
the harbor and you are fortunately not
on it but sitting at the café eating
crab cakes and salad, holding your drink,
cooling the burned skin on your arms under the
umbrella and the sand on the sidewalk slides
like the sand under the Apaches' horses
as they gallop across the desert chasing
the stagecoach and someone has burned the ferry
so they all battle the tumbling river,

the horses struggling up to their necks in the
rushing and my arms are soaked 'cause I'm washing
the dishes. It is important that the house
be in order before night wrestles me to
the ground and the loneliness takes me for a
long ride I may not want to go on – but I
might go – now there is no dialogue in the
movie, just the sky and its rolling cities
of clouds, the tiny coach, six people jammed inside and – for a long time – there is no sound except the music, playing, inexplicably,

– *Nancy Rullo* –

"I Dream of Jeannie with the Light Brown Hair," o-
ver and over – this is material for
a poem, the whole afternoon, if someone...
I watch them watch each other. Wayne mulls the whore,
the gambler ogles the good wife who pats her
damp brow. Her loneliness is withering. Doc
holds the whiskey salesman's display case like some
fine picnic basket he will share with everyone at a cabana in an oasis
in the desert – I watch the sky behind the
stagecoach. I'm the only one who notices

the acrobatics of smoke signals that look
like clouds and not like language –
    Xerxes wept aloud while reviewing his
troops realizing that in one short century,
even the youngest men, clean-cheeked and hearty
child-men will have crumbled with age or collapsed
in battle, their young red blood pumping onto
a field where olives may grow the next year. And
Wayne is dead – lung cancer – and I will be sixty
years old soon – and what will fence me in from time?
Oh give me land, lots of land – anyone's land –

under any skies above – don't fence me in.
Let me write all the wide open stories that
I love, because the best poems are like the songs
I learned to read when I was four, in the Hit
Parade magazine published every week, while
I lay fevered in my perennial or
at least weekly sick bed, the aunts teaching me
melodies while they waited for the men who
battled wars I could not then imagine. I
wheezed along while they smoked Chesterfields and sang

– *Prima Materia* –

to me in my tent of steam, about gazing

at the moon, and now that I have finally
lost my senses I see those songs as my first
poems, black bones galloping across the page
like Apaches with their words of smoke, ducking
the bullets because they didn't want to die then,
or ever perhaps – no one thinks to ask them
what they want or why – but I don't want to die,
though I'm having another drink with the doc,
which is like leaving the fence open – broken
down by wild animals – and death is out there,
somewhere, singing perhaps, but surely smoking,

pulling in that big breath, filling itself with
clouds, with fire, with life and there are no boundaries
especially today when you left to buy
fencing and gates for the garden we wandered
in this morning, but I was alone even
then and when you left it snowed – outside the west
window it hurtled down onto the deck in
a fury of winter and outside the south
window it floated up in thick tongues of spring,
blossoms of snow like signals I couldn't read
because I don't smoke now. I loved my smoke.

Dallas the whore is now in love with John Wayne;
the soldier's wife is sickly and collapses;
suddenly she will produce a fat baby
and no one noticed she is nine months pregnant.
Together Doc and Dallas save her life – and
the little babe is a girl whose cries sound so
much like wolves outside that everyone is confused.
But no one is in here to listen to me.

— *Nancy Rullo* —

I may never know what my cries sound like —
and I can't see whether the damn snow is still
coming down or whether I am living in

a cloud of.... I will not write about damn smoke,
so as I type this madness about a film
I shove some food into my mouth. (I almost
wrote moth — well, I did write moth but I changed it
to mouth — what would I shove into a moth?) Rice
this time and more vodka to wash it down. It's
happy hour somewhere in the world, perhaps
it's time for a drink just up the road apiece.
That's where we all live, all of us, up the road
apiece, up the road from nowhere, where the snow
stops and the sun crawls through the window before

the next squall. In the way out yonder I can
see the mountains rise around me like a fence.
I know what is being walled in and walled out.
Reason has eloped with my intelligence.
They are trotting lazily across a dude
ranch on a honeymoon from my body which
is completely out of control — but in a
feeble attempt to control this "poem" to make
it into something acceptable for the fine
journals, (though as Andre Dubus says: at a
certain point you look at what you are writing

and you say, "Well, there goes the New Yorker,") at
this point, I begin to imagine there might
be a sestina somewhere in here — six words:
smoke stagecoach smoke loneliness smoke loneliness,
but the poem refuses its limits, curls
itself around me and I smell its ashy

— Prima Materia —

fever, its flaring breath. And now you're home with
new fencing for your herbs, and bitter herbs they
will be, to bring me to my knees, to keep me
sober and healthy and writing away inside my fence,
and this is a glimpse of the heartbreaking end

of the poem. I'm having another drink
with the doc and I'm still not smoking. But wait!
A gang of three men in black hats is waiting
for Ringo the Kid when the stagecoach gets to
town — WILL this ever end? The movie, the poem,
the loneliness, the afternoon like a long
trail with dust, sand and smoke in my face, my nose,
my eyes. Why else all these tears? All the whores,
there were many in town, ran to hide. In the
saloon the bartender removed the mirror
from behind the bar, deputies dove into

the jailhouse and Dallas waited for her man
within the murmur of the cottonwood trees,
anticipating a lifelong loneliness.
I don't need to tell you about the ending,
how John Wayne whupped all the bad guys in black hats;
yup, the bad guys died and the good guys lived, and a
few so-so guys were reformed. Doc saved Mr.
Peacock from an arrow in the chest and thence
foreswore the bottle. They went off to Kansas
together, where they will write lovely tracts on
silage and sunflowers. Ringo the Kid and

Dallas the Whore will spend their lives together
on the wrong side of the tracks and grow herbs in
a tub. Their best writing will be some country
songs that no one covers. The good wife went off

– *Nancy Rullo* –

with the grey-faced women from the temperance
union and her poems were notes in her Bible.
I no longer remember what happened to
those Apaches riding off toward different
buttes, lonesome-like on their pied ponies with sand
flying up behind them as they whirled across
that sweet desert. Some of them lived, though, I want

to believe, and they still have their goddamned smoke.
It rises from that smoldering on the hill
and wraps itself around them – the odors sink
into their shirts and hair, the small circles of
smoke swell as they lift, gesturing. "Warning!" they
cry out: "Warning!" and still the circles, the puffs, widen
and thin until they are but a wild glittering
against the sky, a lonesome squall of words
that never lose meaning and the Apache blankets rise
and fall, above the fire, rise and fall. I
breathe it in and sleep.

Deirdre Goes On Dancing

Patrick Hyland

She sips hesitantly from the glass. She does not drink wine as a rule but feels she should in order to please David, the sponsor of what she is certain is going to be an extravagant meal. Deirdre has not been on a date since she met her husband six years before this. There is a large difference between the date she had then and the date she is having now. The dates with Larry were beer and hamburgers most times and when it was within his means, a steak at Jack Dempsey's with martinis. And always the dancing. She doesn't feel there will be any dancing with David. He doesn't seem the type: he likes to play and he likes to work. She knows about both, especially the "play". Since Larry's death David has been after her constantly to go out with him, even before his divorce.

But now that David's marriage is over and she has depleted every excuse in her archive of refusals to him, she agrees with some skepticism to join him for dinner. In contrast, she readily and eagerly accepted Larry's invitation when he approached her that day a half-dozen years ago and suggested a few beers after work. She was not prepared for Larry then, just as she is not prepared for David now.

Next to her, if there was anything Larry loved it was "swing" music and Latin music and a place that would allow them to dance—the jitterbug, the samba, the mambo. On Sundays they would head out to Coney Island for Tito Puente or Prez Prado. Larry had all the moves and if you took away his blond hair and his fair complexion you would not guess that he was a Norwegian on those dance floors. They always arrived in plenty of time for the first dance and stayed until the last, till the lights went out. They were white dots in the crowd then. On Friday's it was to Roseland for Harry James or Jimmy

Dorsey or the like. And the jitterbug, the moves he had and the style he had! Double overhand twirls on the intro, then a pass behind him. At the bridge his arm went around her waist pulling her close to him for a trip around the floor, then stop and swing her to his knee for a few beats, then the other knee. For the coda he tossed her in the air and between his legs then back to a double overhand and finish with a double dip on the final downbeat. Larry brought her along gradually and she loved it and she was good at it. No. More than "good," she was "great" at it! Larry said so. In two months she went from an uncontrollable bag of sand in his hands to a feather in his arms. Other dancers would stop just to watch them, women would come up and ask him to dance. But Larry would decline and put both arms around her waist and gnaw playfully at the nape of her neck and make some remark that he only danced with "his girl." Words like that made her shiver, not with cold but with excitement. In her own eyes, she was nothing special; mousy brown hair, hazel eyes, her nose too small, teeth that could use some straightening, but a body made to dance—she was slender with long legs, graceful arms and hands, shoulders and hips equal widths for the perfect center of gravity, excellent posture, and a waist Larry could almost touch his fingers around. So when Larry said "his girl" like that to other women, she was tempted to say she loved him. But she would wait before she would use a word like that, out loud anyway. They kissed of course, but never petted. Once in a while he might brush up against her breast with his hand, but it always seemed so accidental that it was difficult for her to determine the intention. If he ever decided to touch her she would not protest, she would respond the way she did on the dance floor—willingly, without resistance—whether they were married or not. In those early months he began to occupy more and more of her thoughts. She tried to visualize his life, a subject he skimmed over casually: a high school dropout to get into World War Two before it was over while he still had a chance to get a piece of the glory, then the A-bomb tests on Eniwetok, then his discharge, a few semesters at NYU on the

GI Bill, and then the recall to Korea and six months having his insides surgically rearranged from four thirty-caliber machine gun bullets on Hill 454. Larry told her his doctor said that he would live to be a hundred and fifty. Doctor Gleason had told him that he had low blood pressure and was thirty pounds under weight. After about six months Larry wondered out loud to her one day, what kind of music they would be dancing to a hundred and twenty-five years from then. She shrugged at his silliness and leaned into him. Then he repeated his wonder to her again, "what will we be dancing to a hundred and twenty-five years from now, I'm asking?" She looked at him, he was smiling. Did he mean what she thought he meant? "Get me?" he asked, studying her. "You mean...?" she asked, her pulse climbing higher and higher. "Yeah, that's what I mean," he said, "what do you say?" "I say," she said, "I say, I never thought that I could ever be any happier than I am now, but now I know that's not true anymore. Now I know I can be ecstatically happy, so I say yes, yes, yes, yes, yes!"

"Deirdre?" David says to her, mulling over the wine list, "Are you okay?"

"Of course. Why?" she asks.

"I've asked three times where you got that dress. It's absolutely stunning."

Her dress is black. Black silk, a remnant of fabric she picked up on sale at Macy's for three dollars a yard, ten times what she normally pays, but she couldn't resist. Normally the store doesn't allow remnants to be put on lay-away, but since Deirdre is such a good customer, the clerk puts it away for her anyway. There aren't a lot of people making their own clothes these days the clerk tells her. Religiously, she shows up every Saturday and hands over three dollars until the four and a half yards are paid for. On the fourth Saturday the clerk throws in the half yard for nothing Deirdre discovers and races home with her prize. She can not wait to make this silk into a dress and feel its soft luxury flowing around her body. The pattern she bought for this dress has a simple neckline just over her clavicle with a gore in the back to slip her head through; full-length sleeves blouse over French cuffs that she will use gray satin for. She will also add to the pattern a vertical stripe of this gray satin down the center of the bodice and run two pleats on either side of it to allow about an inch of the gray to show against the black. The waist is simple and straightforward. She thinks about using gray satin for this also, but decides against it. She will wear a belt with it, something with a pearl buckle. The skirt is pleated and will cost a fortune to clean she knows, but she doesn't care. She wears a medium strand of faux pearls from Woolworth's on this date with David—just long enough to break over the neckline—and inserts matching cuff links. A silver-plated peacock pin Larry gave her for her twenty-second birthday sits just above her left breast. Shoulder pads are halfway in fashion and halfway out. Deirdre has put them in. She likes the angle they create from her shoulders down to her waistline.

"I made it myself," she says, wondering if David is staring at the pin on her breast or the breast itself. She lifts the napkin from her lap and dabs her lips and watches his eyes shift back to the wine list.

"Not on company time, I hope," he says.

"No David. Don't worry. They pay me enough to buy my own sewing machine at least."

"Just kidding. C'mon Deirdre, loosen up will you?"

"I have to keep in mind that I am labor and you are management."

"We go back too far to let that come between us I hope."

"I never know."

"Well, what do think this date is all about? Business?"

"I'm sorry. I'm not too good at this I suppose. It's been a while."

"It has? I'm surprised. You mean dating, don't you? All the times you've turned me down, I thought you might be seeing someone. It's been four years since, well, since."

"Larry died?" she asks, filling in the blank.

"Yeah. Sorry, I don't mean to be morbid. It's just that it hasn't been any fault of mine that you haven't been out on the town once in a while."

"But you were married, David. I could never feel comfortable about something like that."

"Well, there's a lot you don't know about my marriage Deirdre and if you want, I'll tell you. But it's only my side. Sylvia has hers no doubt."

"I'll take a pass, okay?"

"That's a deal. There's North Sea salmon on the menu if that suits you and I see they have a '47 Batard-Montrachet on the list. Hell of a wine. I had a bottle in London two years ago. Or there's the filet mignon and a really great '37 Gevery-Chambertin. I doubt there's much of that around anymore. Or go anyway you want, I'm just trying to coordinate the wines if we can. Any suggestions?"

"I've always been a beer and burger girl, David. You know, the bowling alley type so to speak. I wouldn't know a Batard-Monwhatever or a Zhevry-Shemberland from a cherry phosphate. So you decide. Make it your evening. Make it the way you want it."

"Hey, let's back up a second. Maybe it looks like I'm trying to show off or something, but I just want this to be a good thing for you so we can do it again. Often. So if you're not comfortable here, then let's go find a bowling alley. Hell, I was a pin-boy for more years than I want to remember. Still carry a scar where I caught a seven-pin behind my left ear. What do you say? If you're happy I'm happy. There's a lot you don't know about me, Deirdre."

There is a lot David doesn't know about her either, she says to herself while he orders the salmon and the wine. And she wonders what he would think of her if he did. He knows, probably, that she is from upstate, that she graduated in the middle of her high school class with a major in Home Economics, dropped out of Junior College after one semester. He does know that she is a magician with a sewing machine, that she is the forelady of the custom uniform department and that she still pays her union dues. He should know this, he is the Chief Operating Officer of the small garment company they work for in Chelsea where she is also the shop steward. But he does not know that her mother is a drunk and that her father doesn't care and that he works nights tending a loom in a carpet mill. He does not know that she never had a steady boyfriend, until she met Larry, or that she never had a date for her junior or senior prom. Events she attended anyway, just to wear the dresses she had made for herself. And there are other things David doesn't know about her.

David is not aware that she conspired (in her opinion) with Larry's doctor to overdose him with morphine; to suffocate him and send him peacefully to dust. She has always hoped that it was peaceful, but she did not pray that it was peaceful. She did not pray that it was peaceful because she did not want to broach this incident with God, not just then, maybe sometime later. Doctor Gleason had said it was all over, all but the dying at least and the dying wasn't that far in the future; the very last stages. He told her how he would perform this procedure and talked as if Larry was just some sick dog or cat and that she and Larry would both be better off for it. Yes, the doctor who, toward the end, segued from "How are you doing today Mrs Gustavson" into "for the love of Christ, Mrs Gustavson, how long are you going to let him suffer?" That's what perked up her ears—so close to the end: For the love of Christ. Larry's doctor had never put it to her that way before and she knew that was not the context in which he meant it, but it was that tiny loophole she needed that would allow her to live with herself—or so she thought at the time. So she said it. She said: "Yes. Go ahead. Do it." Yes, for the love of Christ, she would be able to confess it now. But she didn't confess it and never has. She still lugs this transgression of hers to confession every Sunday but cannot somehow let the words pass through her lips.

And how would David feel about her if he knew how she hated all those months of endless weeknights and weekends, hour after hour sitting there next to her husband watching him shrivel down to half the skinny man he was to begin with, chewing her nails to the quick, sighing every other breath, staring at the tubes in him; staring at all those pages of all those magazines that might as well have been blank; staring at the photograph of Niagara Falls; staring at the sunken cheeks from where they had pulled all his beautiful teeth, staring at those drooling lips that never spoke; the glassy eyes that blinked on rare occasion and looked at the ceiling; waiting anxiously for the nurse to come in and tell her that visiting hours were over; waiting to breathe again and all the while their friends telling her what a brave lady she was, what a saint she was, how lucky Larry was to have a wife like her?

David will never know that she began to have secret longings for Martin Cassidy who did the six o'clock news on the television she rented to help her through the visits. And how after she couldn't go home and rub herself between her legs to Larry's image any longer, she began to weave Martin into her fantasies under the seclusion of her blanket. David will never know how disgusted she eventually felt about her duplicity. But she thinks that Larry does know this. Yes, just how would David feel if he knew these things? she wonders, while he is talking about buying the company from Manny next year when he retires.

Nor will she ever tell David that she came home from work for more than a year and set the table for Larry and prepared dinner for him and talked to him as if he were sitting right there in the kitchen with her, a bottle of beer in his hand. She can't tell David that she would report to Larry when she reached her production bonus and how the extra money would go well toward a house and topics like that. It's true, she would actually talk out loud to Larry and tell him about his brother and how his niece and nephew were growing up. She recited the letters she wrote to his parents about how she was getting on in her job and about her promotion and how much she loved and missed their son. She had no doubt that Larry was aware of all those things, but it felt better to her if she said them out loud, so she could hear them herself, so the rooms would fill with some sound of human activity, with the day-to-day, with nothing important. Sometimes she would bring out the photo albums for him and see a snapshot that would make her laugh and ask him if he remembered. And after dinner, she would put on the records and she would dance. She would dance the slow dances feeling him press close to her, feeling his lips on her ear.

There is plenty that David doesn't know. He doesn't know that she feels as if Larry is always around her, watching and listening. He is around when she is awake, when she is asleep, watching in some extrasensory silence, hovering over her every move, prying into every thought she has, watching her make the coffee in the morning, watching her deposit her subway tokens, watching her decide between the pastrami or the ham salad in the deli, even watching her and David that very moment, listening to David say something about moving the company South and something else about labor costs and taxes as he motions for the waiter to bring the dessert menu.

David does not know that she wakes during the night, every night, and sees a glow by the bedroom door. It is not a human image, nothing like that, just a white, oblong, radiating gleam that shrinks to a small white dot when she whispers, "Larry? Are you here?" After the first few nights of that, she taped the shade to the window frame just to make sure that it was not a reflection or light leaking through from the streetlights. And after she did this, she found that the glimmer was still there. It will be present tonight when she returns, she knows it. She doubts she will ever be able to tell David this part either (if things should work out between them), and then David says something about what an asset she can be when he takes over the company and how her department is the only profit center they have these days. He says that she is the most gorgeous woman he has ever been with in his life.

Until now she has been confident that he has been honest with her, but this last comment makes her skeptical and wary. He continues that he has missed his train out to Long Island to spend Saturday with his children. He says he has been sleeping in the office for months until a deal on a co-op he has his eyes on goes through. He says he is tired of this and wonders if she could put him up for the night. Just this one night, he pleads. She says that it is not a good idea. And he says something about: not on the first date, huh? And she responds with: not on any date Buster and take your hand off my wrist you shithead and walks out with the maitre'd looking puzzled and his mouth open and David shouting behind her that she has him all wrong. David is no dancer she thinks to herself, slamming through the brass door.

Outside the shows are letting out over on Forty Second and she rushes across Eighth and loses herself in the crowd, hopefully to thwart any attempt of David's to follow her. Then she heads down to Thirty-fourth and goes underground there instead of Times Square.

It is a good ride up to One Hundred and Tenth from there and even though seats are available she prefers to stand and feel the rhythm of the ride come up through her legs, her hips. Maybe she'll get off at Ninety-sixth and just stroll up Broadway. She has the need for a walk, to let some of the evening blow off her, maybe a beer at the Dive Bar over on Commercial with some small talk before she goes back to the flat. She doesn't want to carry the crap with David to the place where she and Larry have had so much happiness together. The place where his medals are and things that meant something to him: the Bronze Star, the Purple Heart, the Good Conduct Medal, the Division patches, his Honorable discharge, all framed on red velvet, his letter of commendation for his participation in the A-Tests on Eniwetok. There are the books too; novels mostly—Steinbeck, Hemingway, DeMaurier, O'Hara, Spillane, others, nothing too lofty though. And the photographs: his parents, his brother and his family, her parents on one of their good days, her in a communion dress, her at graduation from PS Ten, her at graduation from Edison High, the two of them at Rockaway with Larry so thin and her in a one piece; their wedding picture in front of City Hall; Larry in Nagasaki, Larry on Eniwetok Atoll, Larry at Inchon, all in fatigues, those haunting eyes searching back at her through the times before she knew him.

Going through the motions now, up the stairs out on to Broadway, passing the diner, just walking, taking deep breaths, calming herself, she buys a sack of apples at the fruit stand then walks over to Commercial, enters the Dive Bar and has a Schaeffer's on tap. The Rangers won tonight, the barkeep says and she says it's about time. And another thing David doesn't know, she continues to herself. He doesn't know that Larry is the only man she has ever made love with and that she has troubling fears about lying down with another man. He does not know that she has heard the women at work tell the stories of what goes on in their beds, the brutality, the lack of consideration, the selfishness, some of the perversities. For every two stories like that there is one story like her story. Larry was tender and caring. If she wasn't ready, he was patient. If she was ready, he was gentle. She would lose count of the number of times he told her he loved her when they touched and then he would hold her for the longest time when it was over and kiss her until she slept. She could not tell the other women these things about Larry. Most of them would not believe her. Maybe a few would.

The barkeep wants to know if he will see her tomorrow as she finishes her second beer and she says only if it rains. She decides she will take the bus to Rockaway if it is decent out and if it isn't maybe she'll go anyway and just walk the beach in the rain. She likes Rockaway in the rain, dancing away from the surf, just her and Larry except for the sand pipers darting in front of her, teasing her.

She crosses One Hundred and Tenth and feels a blister forming on her heel from the new shoes she has bought to go with her new dress and wants to hurry before she can't walk any longer. By the time she gets to Amsterdam the blister overwhelms her and she walks the last three blocks in her stocking feet. Holes begin to appear through the nylon and pull tight on her toes, cutting into them. Larry is close to her now, she can feel it. She can almost smell him, he is so close. He

— Prima Materia —

watches her press the number four button in the elevator and he sees that she is crying and that she has lost her sack of fruit and that she has only one shoe in her hand; the other is somewhere back on the sidewalk by the empty paper bag, and the apples are rolling into the gutter. He sees her unlock the door and undress. She does not hang everything neatly as she usually does. She throws her clothing on the floor as if it is contaminated and jumps into bed. Yes, Larry is there, she can feel his sighs on the back of her neck and behind her ear. She is in their bed where she is safe and she waits for sleep.

She has a dream and it is a wonderful dream. She has not had this dream before. There is a long deserted wharf except for some lobster boats on each side slowly rocking on the incoming tide. It is a warm evening and Deirdre moves along it in a lavender nightgown; she is fascinated by the cloud formations silhouetted against a dusky gray horizon to the east. A gentle breeze strokes her as she pirouettes on tiptoes toward the end of the wharf, lowering and lifting her arms as if she is about to soar. She is concerned about the bare wood beneath her feet though and the splinters that she might incur. This concern inhibits her desire to dance with the wild abandon she would like to. She doesn't want to care about things right now, she just wants to twirl and laugh and dance. Faint innocent whimpers of what seems to be a puppy whining somewhere nearby eases her concern but still she keeps cautious of the splinters, the innocent sound of the puppy gives her comfort and a feeling that she is not alone. How glorious it is. The freedom and the peace that is there, the hollow gurgles of the tide against the boat hulls, the occasional shrill pipe of a gull above. The puppy appears after a while, nipping playfully at her heels, a fluffy blond thing with affectionate dark eyes and a teasing smile. Its tail wags when she laughs. She whirls childlike, the puppy nipping at her dancing feet. Then something begins to hurt around her heel and she feels something sharp clamp to her ankle. Looking behind to check herself, she sees the puppy is no longer there and blood is pouring down her leg on to the wood planks. A piece of her flesh about the size of a walnut has been torn away and is hanging by a thin sliver of skin. Another dog, a massive adult, its head almost up to her chest, has somehow risen in the puppy's place and purposefully steps toward her baring its teeth, lips trembling, the blond fur raised high on its back. It lunges at her and tears at her gown, bracing itself against the planking and her struggle to pull away. She must get to the water, she will be safe there. But as the dog pulls at her, she feels other bites ripping at her, other dogs jumping on her, sharp nails clawing into her back. There are more dogs, how many she cannot count, they grin at her and howl and fight each other in some sort of frenzied competition to get their fair share of her. Two of the dogs, then three, fight over her gown, shredding it at the seams. Naked now, she runs toward the end of the wharf and more dogs pummel her, tearing at her hair and her cheeks, their teeth sinking deep into her arms and her breasts; their breath nauseates her. She crumbles under the weight of them. The lead dog, its penis in arousal, has knocked her down and is poking at her, its jaws around her throat. She feels him enter her. "No. Please, no," she screams, and claws her way slowly toward the edge of the wharf, giving up her flesh to them until she is close enough to plunge into the cold water. The salt stings at her open wounds; she is blind in the water's darkness, unable to sink much below the surface. Choking, she rises to the top. The tide moves slowly and steadily and carries her toward shore. The dogs now pace back and forth along the beach sniffing the air for the scent of her. One by one they enter the surf and paddle rhythmically toward her, the tide rapidly closing the distance between them.

"Larry help me, please help me," she shouts into the darkness and wakes to find she is sitting upright panting rapidly, gasping. The bedclothes are soaked with her perspiration; residuals of the dream still flash before her. She lies there, assessing herself, her arms, her breasts, her thighs, her whole body smarts from the assaults. She is shocked when she discovers that she is nude and blushes for some reason unknown to her. Frantically she searches for her gown and tears the covers back, but there is no sign of it. She feels for it under the bed and under the mattress. She tosses the pillows. She flings her clothes from the drawers and from the closet but her gown is nowhere to be found.

She lies down again, her breathing beginning to slow. She turns her head toward the bedroom door but the glow she expects is not there. She has slept through it. It will not return tonight. Her gown will be somewhere, she is sure. She will find it in the morning.

"Larry? Are you here?" she whispers and pauses as if she expects him to respond. She always pauses as if he will respond.

"Larry, I never meant you any harm," she says. She always says this to him.

She always closes her eyes and she always waits. And then slowly, always slowly, she goes on dancing.

Can You Forgive Me, Pumpkin?

Irene McGarrity

For the past three weeks, whenever Karen and George worked together on the same shift at McDonald's of New Paltz, she gave him a ride home in her 1982 Nova. It wasn't that George didn't have a car of his own, but the inspection had expired. And when George had taken it to get inspected at the Fleet Auto Center, the mechanic told him that there was a special part he needed. He could never remember the name of the part, or where it went in the car, or why it was so important, even though the mechanic had thoroughly explained all of these things to George. He could only remember that it cost five hundred dollars, not including labor. So George was saving up. There was an old friend of his father's that worked at the Sunoco Service Station. He would have given him a new inspection sticker for one hundred dollars. But he was only in the shop on Tuesdays from 10 AM until 2 PM and George was in school at that time. Also, he felt there was something dishonest about it. He liked the idea of saving up money to buy something that he needed. His father would have never understood that though. He came home from work every Tuesday night and cracked open a can of Coors Light. He'd say, "Ya get the car done, Georgie?"

George would say, "No, Dad. I had to go to school today."

His dad would say, "Are ya still in school, Georgie? Christ, I thought you'd be done with all that nonsense by now." And that's how it was in George's house.

He liked riding home with Karen anyway. The inside of her Nova always smelled like cinnamon. George thought it smelled like a little baker lived in the trunk and made cinnamon rolls all day long. Even the greasy smell from their uniforms disappeared in her car. Also, George was in love with Karen. He had been for as long as he knew her, but the rides home over the past three weeks had made the love feelings stronger. His heart had puffed up and gotten bigger like all of those cinnamon rolls.

Karen pulled her seat belt over her and clicked it into place. She waited for George to do the same thing with his seat belt. She winked at him the way she always did before turning the key in the ignition. "Ready?" she said.

George said, "You got it, sister." It was part of their little routine. Karen pulled out onto Route 299 and George looked out the window. He was enjoying the smell of cinnamon and the view of the 87 Motel and the Mobil station. In his mind, he said, *So would you want to catch a movie sometime?* That was also part of their three-week routine, only Karen didn't know about that part. He felt her hand fumbling around for the little tape recorder that sat between them. She used it to play music in her car because the radio was broken. Karen only owned three tapes. She alternated between The B52s, Cindy Lauper, and Simon and Garfunkel. Karen's hand brushed against George's leg and he heard the click of the Play button. He was expecting to hear "Scarborough Fair" or "True Colors," but instead a deep, scratchy voice filled up the car. It said, "I don't know if I told you this one or not. Maybe I told your sister or your brother—but listen, there's a priest, a garbage man, and a guy dressed up as Santa Claus..."

George heard the little button click again. "Sorry," said Karen. "I forgot I was listening to my dad's tape on the way to work." The car felt hot. It felt like heat was emanating from Karen's cheeks. George smiled at this thought, at the thought of her pink cheeks warming up the car. He liked the idea of it the same way he liked the idea of saving up for that special part, whatever it was called. They turned down North Ohioville and then down Oaktown Road.

George said, "Your dad makes tapes of himself talking to you?"

Karen said, "Yeah. Kind of like how people write letters?"

"Oh," he said. "That's pretty nice."

"Yeah," she said. "He lives in California."

They were quiet for a while, listening to car sounds. "We can listen to it if you want," said George. "I'm kind of curious about that joke."

She laughed. "He's not going to tell it."

George said, "What do you mean?"

Karen said, "Look. Watch." She turned the tape player on.

"...and you know, they're all havin' a drink together at this night club...and um...what was it? Oh—no wait...was it Santa Claus or a guy in a rabbit costume? Oh forget it..."

George and Karen laughed and they listened to the tape some more while they talked.

"He always does that," she said. "He's always starting to tell jokes and forgetting them."

George laughed and looked at her smile about her dad. He liked the way the street lamps lit up her face every few blocks. He liked the way a piece of her hair rested on her forehead.

"...Yeah, your sister's a pisser sometimes..."

They turned down Plutarch Road and George thought, *Maybe we could catch a flick one of these days.* He said, "Your dad sounds like a nice guy."

Karen said, "He is. He's wonderful."

"...the way me and your mom used to take turns bringing you kids out to the park..."

– Prima Materia –

George thought about his own dad. He couldn't imagine him saying things into a tape recorder and sending them to him in the mail. He couldn't imagine him in California.

"...You kids, I swear, always into some kind of new scheme to get me and your mom to stay together. It was a real trip..."

George felt the heat from Karen's cheeks again. He thought, *Would you and your cheeks like to accompany me to the movies one day?* They were pulling into George's driveway and he saw his uninspected car. He pictured his dad inside, waiting for him in front of the television with a can of Coors Light resting on his knee. *Get that car inspected today, Georgie?* He closed his eyes and thought. He thought about asking Karen to the movies. He knew he wouldn't ever do it, no matter how long his car sat there. No matter how many times his father asked him about it.

"...I feel like...I don't know..." There was a silence and then a clicking sound and then a deep breath. Her dad had lit a cigarette. "I never told you this, pumpkin, and it bugs me.... I didn't mean to...I mean...but you were crying and I didn't know what to do..."

George fumbled around in the seat, pretending to look for his keys. Karen's cheeks were burning the car up.

"...and your mom was out, God knows where and I just lost it. I started shaking you and—." His voice broke. He was crying and George felt Karen's hand fumbling around for the little tape recorder. "—You stopped breathing for a few seconds. It scares the shit out of me and I still have nightmares about—." The tape clicked off. Karen was still for a minute, staring straight ahead. George did the same. He figured the best way to make her comfortable was to do exactly what she did. He stared at his Plymouth Duster. He squinted and tried to see the expired sticker, but of course he couldn't.

"I'm sorry you had to hear that, George," she said finally. "My dad never says things like that on his tapes. He always talks about my brother and sister and starts to tell jokes and never finishes them and—." Her voice broke the same way her father's had. She was sniffling and heating the car at the same time. George looked at her. She was more beautiful than he had ever seen her before. And he thought of all the rides they had shared together. He thought of all the nights he had lain in bed, staring up at the ceiling, thinking about her. He thought of all the times he had changed the schedule at McDonald's when no one was looking so that they could work together and ride home in Karen's cinnamon-mobile. "It's okay." He said. George patted her on the back and she nodded and cried. Her coat made a swishing noise under his hand. He said, "Karen, would you want to go to a movie or something one of these days?" It wasn't how he had planned to say it at all. He just sort of blurted it out. She stopped crying for a few seconds and looked at him. Her eyes were wide and the tears made them shiny. Karen turned away and started to sob. George pulled back from her. He thought he must have offended her in some terrible way. He must have said the worst possible thing he could have said at that moment. "I'm sorry," he said. "I'm sorry. You don't have to ever drive me home again. I'm an idiot." He opened the car door and began to get out. Then something strange happened. Something that George would have never expected. She pulled him back towards her by his coat and the passenger-side door slammed shut. She kissed him. She kissed him in a way that George didn't think girls were capable of. She held on to him and he felt her lips and her tongue and he felt her tears against his cheek. Karen finally let go of him and they looked at each other. She said, "I'd love to." She must have seen how confused George looked. "I mean go to the movies with you some time."

"Really?" His voice squeaked and he cleared his throat. "Really?"

"Sure," she said.

George said, "Okay." And they were both back to staring straight ahead. George squinted and tried to look at the sticker again as if the kiss could have improved his vision. He tried to remember the name of that part, but of course he couldn't.

Karen said, "Well, I better get home."

"Oh," said George. "Okay." He opened the car door and said, "Goodnight."

She said, "Goodnight, George."

He pretended to go around to the back door, but he just stood there behind a tree. George wanted to let the kiss settle on his lips before he went inside and saw his father. He didn't want there to be any chance that his father would take that kiss away before it had a chance to sink into his skin.

Karen hadn't pulled out of the driveway yet. George turned around and spied on her from behind the tree. He saw her roll down the window of the car and toss her McDonald's hat in the back seat. She pulled something from the sun visor. It was a pack of cigarettes and she lit one up. She exhaled the smoke and stared straight ahead for a minute. Then he saw Karen reach for something beside her and he knew what she was doing. George strained his ears and he could just barely make out her father's voice. "Can you forgive me, pumpkin? Do you think you can forgive an old man like me?"

Meetings in the Spaces Between

The Cognate Café

Isaac Weiner

A stranger wandered into the Cognate Café on a Sunday night. It was a nice place with many-paneled windows. White Christmas tree lights glittered from inside, shining like beacons in the mist that had settled around the café and along the highway that ran perpendicular to it.

The stranger did not drive up. The dirt parking lot had three cars in it, two white and one green.

The café was painted light green with white trim. It was a renovated house with a style that suggested 1800s but was quietly modern. On the side of the house opposite the highway, there was a shallow yet wide river that was dotted with large rocks and boulders worn smooth on the bottom by the rushing water. The dry areas of these rocks were sharp with minute crags.

When the stranger opened the door to the café, a bell jangled. He stopped at the entrance and quickly scraped his wet and muddy shoes on the welcome mat, having forgotten to do so outside. The one waitress in the café looked at him for a short period of time and then dropped her eyes a few moments before she knew he would raise his.

He looked around. The floor of the café was wood, waxed and mopped and shining brightly. It looked clean. The tables were wood as well, and the chairs were wooden and painted white, with patterned cushions. There was a flower in each vase on each table even though it was winter. The tabletops were not shiny like the floor; they were natural and solid. The tables were bolted to the floor. The walls were wainscoted about a third of the way up in dark green and the walls were plaster in light green, with white trim again. There were no chairs at the counter, which was very clean and stocked with coffee-producing machines, and coffee, and coffee-related items. Behind the counter an open doorway led to the kitchen, which could not be seen.

A big man in a plaid shirt sat at one of the tables, drinking coffee. He had hair that was almost red, and small eyes. His rolled-up shirtsleeves revealed bear-like arms. He nodded at the stranger.

The stranger nodded back. He walked forward and sat down at a table to his left, a table with two chairs. The big man was sitting far to his right, facing towards the door—in the opposite direction. The waitress quietly got together her menu and notepad and pen in a quick, orderly manner and walked over to the stranger.

"Hi," she said.

The stranger saw that she had a very white face with lots of freckles. Her eyes were expectant but tired. She was a young girl, possibly twenty. She had a ponytail and her face was very curved.

"What can I get you?"

"Can I see your menu?"

The big man looked at him. There was a couple at the far side of the café and they turned their heads. They were in their thirties and eating dinner. There was a small exclamation from the kitchen. They all knew he was a stranger now.

"Suuure," said the girl slowly. She had the menu tucked under her arm. She handed it to him. She was unsure as to whether she should walk away or stay there.

"I won't be here long. I think I'll just have coffee. Black coffee."

"Sure." The waitress brought out her fleeting smile and took it back right away. The big man raised his eyebrows as he went back to his coffee and newspaper, and the couple

— *Prima Materia* —

exchanged glances. The stranger tapped his fingers on the table. He looked out the window at a car driving down the highway.

A large, settled woman came out. She looked like an unhealthy female Atlas, perhaps carrying a great weight. She looked at the stranger from the counter, lowering her eyes. She moved slowly beyond the counter and then leaned in front of it.

"Hi there," she said to the stranger.

He looked up. He had black hair and was slightly dirty. His clothes were damp. He was probably in his late twenties. Although she couldn't see, his shoes were scuffed and dirty.

He nodded at her.

"What's your name?" she asked.

"Oh—it's always changing," he laughed. The big man looked at him again. The couple looked at him again. The waitress was somewhere in the kitchen.

"Well, are we just gonna call you stranger, stranger?"

"I guess so."

"So where are you from?"

The stranger's hands could not keep still. They were fiddling with each other now. The others in the café listened.

"I'm from the river." He pointed in the direction of the big man.

"Is that so," said the large woman. She folded her arms. The girl came out with the stranger's coffee and quickly walked over to his table with it. She set it down before him and began walking back towards the kitchen. She stopped and changed her mind. She could not simply walk back, or stay where she was, and she did not apparently want to stand by the large woman. She did not want to lean against a table. She began to look busy with a coffee machine.

"Is this your place?" asked the stranger of the large woman.

"Indeed it is," she replied, smiling affectionately. "I was practically born here. I *was* born here, actually. This place is my life. I like this place." She fondled the counter.

"She *is* this place," said the big man, grinning at the stranger. "She ain't another for life."

"I'll die here," she stated. "I'll know I've run a nice place. This is where I belong."

"I know with who," winked the big man. The woman smiled disapprovingly. She looked at the ceiling, and a few minutes passed. The stranger finished his coffee, and the girl quickly walked over and asked him if he was done with it. He nodded and she took it away, grateful for somewhere to go.

"Think you'll be back, stranger?" asked the woman. The couple had finished eating and was now watching the stranger. They were full and too tired to get up and move on.

"I don't know."

"You going back where you're from?" The woman winked. "The river?"

"I don't think so. I don't usually go to places twice."

"See now," began the woman. "See."

The big man wiped his grin with his napkin. The girl walked over to the couple and she walked stiffly. She asked them if they were done. They nodded and she took away their leftovers but they did not get up or take out their money.

"I was born here, in this place," said the big woman. "This is my place. It always has been, since I first knew it. I know this place well, these tables, and these people. I know my customers, stranger. And I think—actually, I know—that this place, this little café, this little square of land between that highway and that river, is mine. Everyone has some little piece of land—everyone on earth has this piece that belongs to them—no, that they belong to. Just like they all have a person they belong to. And I've been so lucky, stranger, because I've found my place on earth. But you, stranger, where's your place?"

"I don't know. Everywhere. I'm always on the move."

The girl was standing close to the couple's table, waiting for them to take out their money and pay and leave. The man glared at her a little bit but the woman sat blissfully, listening to the larger lady.

"You haven't found your place, stranger. You're a real wanderer, and you haven't found what makes you *human*. Your place is what makes you human, because it makes you *belong*. It's your life."

The stranger got up.

The woman sighed. "Always on the move," she said. She looked at the waitress.

"Clara," she snapped, "leave those people alone to finish their meal."

"They're *finished*," said Clara angrily.

"What's the matter with you now?"

"Here we go," said the big man, shaking his head.

"I want to go home," said Clara.

"See," said the woman. "See. I want to go here. I want to go there. Nobody ever's happy with where they *are*. She can't let those people stay where they are. Why can't we just sit and relax?"

"Thanks for the coffee," said the stranger. "I'm off again."

"I'm going home," said Clara.

"Suits me!" choked the woman. "Go on! You don't belong here anyway! You go off with your stranger! This is my place! Find one of your own!"

The big man and the couple got up simultaneously.

Clara pushed past the stranger as they went out the door. The stranger walked to the edge of the highway and looked both ways.

"Where are you going?" asked Clara, taking out her car keys. "I can take you there."

"No, you can't," said the stranger.

Clara didn't say anything.

"Do you see that river?" asked the stranger, pointing at it. They both looked as it flowed with great speed past the little café.

"Do you see those rocks?" he asked. "I came over on those rocks. They're all sharp on the top. On the bottom though, the river keeps flowing on them, and making them all smooth and round. They get worn down and the river carries them downstream."

Clara shook her head. The stranger took her hand and pulled her towards the river. He stood on the bank and then stretched his foot out towards the closest rock. It wobbled slightly.

"It's almost on its way," he said. Still holding on to her, he stepped onto it in the darkness and then stepped forward again, pulling her with him.

"I can't see," she said. It was dark out, and the only lights were from the café windows.

"That's how it is, often," said the stranger. The rock wobbled and she almost fell into the river.

"No," she gasped.

"It's all right," said the stranger. "That's how it is. That's how it goes. It'll take you. I came from it. It took me."

The rock wobbled again from their combined weight and she gave out a little shriek and then they fell together, in the dark, into the water and the tide carried them downstream, away from the café, into the world.

Six Miniature Fictions

Clark Strand

Feather

On my way to work I saw a small gray feather, the length of a woman's fingernail, twirling in one spot as if held by an invisible shot glass made of air. When after a minute it didn't fall, I walked around it. I don't know if this means anything, but I felt disquiet all that day.

Naked

My small daughter is lying naked on the backdoor steps trying to catch raindrops in her bellybutton. Her eyes are shut, and her concentration is something to behold. Every few moments her belly catches a new one, and she scoots her buttocks further to one side, I presume to make a closer approximation to where the next raindrop will fall. Looking at her lying there, I catch a brief glimpse of myself and wonder if any part of my life is still beautiful.

Loyalty

Loyalty has its price. On the day K. is to meet his fiancée it rains. Nobody, not even God, could have predicted that.

Because it rains, a number of things happen in a not-supposed-to kind of way. K. knows this because of who he is.

When the moment arrives that K.'s fiancée is supposed to trip on the bus step, falling back into his arms, it doesn't happen. She wakes early and takes the first, not the second bus. She takes a window seat, and gazes blankly at Seventh Avenue.

When the bus pulls away from the 59th Street stop, K. has just arrived. Seeing her in the window, he holds his hand up as if to say, "I tried."

His fiancée speaks only with her eyes. The eyes say, "It happens every time."

Nose

Looking in the mirror one morning I noticed that my nose was off. Crooked, by six or seven degrees. I'd taken bearings off it all my life. It was possible that I'd got everything wrong. So I performed the necessary adjustment with my eyes and began the day.

At first I found it difficult to stand. But after a few minutes my balance returned. It was remarkable seeing the world with its crookedness removed. I'd always been unhappy, and now I understood why.

That night I made love to my girlfriend. It was even better than before. But afterward she wouldn't stop crying. "What's the matter?" I asked. She answered, "You don't love me anymore."

Story

A man begging for change asks me for "two bits." I give him a quarter.

Having met with some success, he presses forward. "You know that clock in England?"

"Yeah," I say.

"Once the time was wrong. It was during the war. The Germans did it. I don't know how. Isn't that something?"

"Yeah," I say and hand him another quarter.

"Maybe it made a difference, maybe not," he continues.

I consider this for a moment, then hand him another quarter. But he only stares at me hopelessly. He has reached the end of his story.

Stick

In a dream I saw Gandhi standing by the river. "Here," he said, "hold this for me," and that's how I got this stick.

Contributors

Stories We Tell Ourselves

Marlene Adelstein is a freelance writer and editor of novels and screenplays. She worked for over twenty years as an executive in feature film and television development for: Wind Dancer Films, Fine Line Features, The Zanuck Company, and The Samuel Goldwyn Company. Her short fiction has appeared in *The Madison Review*, *Fine Print*, and *Mars Hill Review*. Marlene has received fellowships to Yaddo, MacDowell Colony, The Wurlitzer Foundation, and Fundacion Valpairiso. She lives in Rosendale. Her Web site is www.marleneadelstein.com.

Duff Allen was born in 1962. He got his B.A. from Middlebury in 1984. He got his M.F.A. from Bard in 1996. He has a teenage son named Nemo. He is madly in love with Carrie Belle Monroe.

Bob Bachner writes fiction and drama in a dungeon in Bearsville and practices law in NYC. He is a director of The Appleseed Foundation, a national organization that creates public interest law centers, and he serves on the national council of Environmental Defense. "Just a Riffle" came out of a trip with ED. He is married to mixed-media artist Barbara Bachner; their daughter, Suzanne, is a writer and producer. His previous credits include two off-off-Broadway productions and one story. He hopes that publication in Prima Materia presages success for his just-completed novel.

Saul Bennett is a new poet, following a business career in New York. Bennett began writing poems to tackle the furies of his grief following the sudden death of his 24-year-old daughter, Sara, from a brain aneurysm in 1994. His first poems appeared in a host of publications, and his first collection, *New Fields and Other Stones/On a Child's Death*, was chosen in 1998 to launch a new publishing imprint, Archer Books, and subsequently received the Benjamin Franklin Silver Award. Bennett's second collection, *Harpo Marx at Prayer*, (Archer Books 2000), was nominated by the publisher for the Pulitzer Prize. He recently a completed a new collection, *Sea Dust*. Bennett and his wife, Joan, live in Woodstock.

Celia Bland's collection of poetry, *Soft Box*, will be published by CavanKerry Press in 2004. She teaches at Bard College.

– *Contributors* –

William Boyle was born and raised in Brooklyn. He has lived in the Hudson Valley for six years. He is currently a Teaching Assistant and student in the English MA program at SUNY New Paltz.

Carl Frankel is a writer, journalist, consultant, and entrepreneur specializing in sustainable development. His current positions include Senior Consultant with the US-based business magazine Green@Work; community liaison with High Ridge on the Hudson LLC, a sustainable community; and membership on the Board of Directors of the Buckminster Fuller Institute. His most recent book, *Out of the Labyrinth: Who We Are, How We Go Wrong, and What We Can Do About It*, will be published by the Rhinebeck-based Monkfish Book Publishing Company in Spring 2004. Frankel lives with his wife Deborah Bansemer in Kingston.

A graduate of Northwestern and Columbia University, **Alison Sloane Gaylin** has covered entertainment and the arts for a variety of publications and Web sites. Her first screenplay, *Unleashed* (co-written with her husband Michael Gaylin) was a finalist in the 2003 Austin Film Festival screenwriting competition. She recently completed her first novel, and lives in Woodstock with her husband, daughter and dog.

Patrick Hyland lives in East Windham, NY with his wife and his fly rods. "By the time I was fifteen I had lived in more cities and towns than I have fingers, thanks to an itinerant father. I attended Johns Hopkins and Northwestern long before there were degrees in creative writing; if there had been, I might have avoided thirty-five years in the advertising business. Now that I am retired, I am doing what I wanted to do when I was twenty-five: live on the side of a mountain and write stories." He attends Writers in the Mountains workshops. "Dierdre..." is his first published story.

Emily Katz is currently a senior at Bard College studying creative writing and literature. She has lived in the Hudson Valley for four years and though she will soon be leaving, expects to return later in her life.

Richard Klin has completed a novel. His writing has appeared in *Forward, Publishers Weekly, Parabola, Moment*, and online at *January* and *LiP*. He lives in Stone Ridge with his wife, painter Lily Prince.

Paloma Julia Rodriguez Kopp, age 12, has been drawing since she was two. She wrote her first comic strip when she was about six, although she did not publish it. Her comics appear occasionally in the *Phoenicia Times*. She attends Phoenicia Elementary School.

Mary Leonard is an Associate of the Institute for Writing and Thinking at Bard College where she teaches workshops and consults. She also teaches every summer in the writing program for high school students at Simon's Rock College. In between teaching gigs, she tries to write and last year published a chapbook, *21st Century Flint*, with 2River. She also sometimes writes for *About Town* and she is working on a novel, tentatively titled *Italian Ice*.

Irene McGarrity lives in High Falls, goes to school in New Paltz, and looks back on her career as a fast food employee with fondness and a little bit of melancholy.

Will Nixon has published two poetry chapbooks: *When I Had It Made* (Pudding House Publications) and *The Fish Are Laughing* (Pavement Saw Press), which won a national chapbook contest. After moving from a Manhattan apartment to a Catskills log cabin in 1996, he wrote a number of personal essays for regional and national magazines, which are now collected at www.mycabinfever.com. His reflections on the Unabomber, which ran in the *North Dakota Quarterly* as "Visions of Kaczynski," was listed as a "Notable Essay" in *The Best American Essays of 2003*.

Philip Pardi has poems in recent or forthcoming issues of *Mid-American Review, Hotel Amerika, Indiana Review, Marlboro Review*, and previously in *Prima Materia*. He lives with his family in a log cabin in the Catskills and teaches at Marist College.

Michael Perkins is the author of five collections of poetry, including the *Blue Woman* (1966), *The Persistence of Desire* (1977), *Praise in the Ears of Clouds* (1982), *Gift of Choice* (1992), and *I Could Walk All Day* (2002). *The Secret Record*, literary criticism, was published by William Morrow

– Contributors –

in 1976. Among his other works of fiction and non-fiction are the novels *Evil Companions* (1968, 1992, 2003), and *Dark Matter* (1996, 2002).

Melissa Holbrook Pierson is the author of *The Perfect Vehicle* and *Dark Horses and Black Beauties*, both from Norton. Although she now lives in Ulster County, she once had a house far into the Catskills, where "Dead End" is set.

Guy Reed's essay, "Father's Day" appears in *My Heart's First Steps*, an anthology published by Adams Media Corporation in October 2003. He has contributed to the *Saugerties Times* as a guest columnist and has been a featured performance poet at many venues in the Mid-Hudson Valley. He lives with his wife, artist Beth Humphrey and their two children in the Catskill Mountains.

Nancy Rullo writes poetry, fiction and nonfiction. She has been an instructor of creative writing at Ulster County Community College, and teaches poetry and essay writing to adults and teenagers in Woodstock. Rullo has also taught at the Hudson Valley Writer's Guild. Recent poems have been published in *Aurorean, Reflect, Blueline, HalfMoon Review, Dream International Quarterly,* and *Tertulia*. Essays have appeared in *The Woodstock Times, Chronogram,* and the book *The Day My Father Died*. Rullo was a semifinalist in the White Pine Coffeehouse Fiction Contest. She is currently at work on *The Odd God*, a series of images and poetry in collaboration with Gay Leonhardt.

Gerald Seligman has published journalism in *Rolling Stone, Billboard, The LA Times, The Village Voice, The Nation* and a host of other newspapers and magazines. He has worked since the late 1980s in the music industry and has lived in Brazil and London, the latter where he created and ran EMI's world music label, Hemisphere. He has been living in the Hudson Valley, near Woodstock, since 2000. He is currently undergoing a novel.

Lorna Smedman is a graduate of the Jack Kerouac School of Disembodied Poetics and the author of *Dangers of Reading* (Prospect Books). One of her stories appeared recently in *Rites of Passage*, an anthology of travel stories published by Lonely Planet. After living in

Manhattan for the past two decades, she is surprised to be the owner of a little stone shack in her hometown in Ulster County.

Sparrow is teaching Personal Magic to young scholars in Phoenicia, NY. His favorite food is chow mein. (Look for his two volumes on www.softskull.com)

Clark Strand has written books on poetry and spirituality and is the author of *How to Believe in God*, forthcoming from Riverhead. An internationally known haiku poet and teacher, he began writing "microfictions" in 1980 after reading early translations of Yasunari Kawabata's "Palm of the Hand Stories." But it was only in 1996, however, after befriending the poet Sparrow, that he began to understand the art of "unbearably short fiction." He lives in Woodstock, with his wife and fellow writer Perdita Finn and their two children.

Isaac Weiner lives in High Falls, NY, and is currently attending St. John's College in Annapolis, MD. "The Cognate Cafe" is his first published work.

Rachel X. Weissman is a writer living in her father's Catskills cabin.

Minda Zetlin is a freelance writer and nonfiction book author. Most recently, she was one of more than 20 authors of *The ASJA Guide to Freelance Writing* (St. Martin's Press, 2003). She's a graduate of the New York University Masters program in Creative Writing, and her fiction has appeared in the journals *Trellis, Ellipsis* and (appropriately) *Unknowns*. "Learning to Jump" is her favorite of all her short stories. She lives in Woodstock with her husband Bill Pfleging, a large number of computers, and four cats.

The universe is made of stories, not atoms.
—*Muriel Rukeyser*

First, last, and always, thanks to Wendy.